THE HUMAN SIDE
OF THE SAINTS

Studies of Old Testament
Personalities

*CONTEMPORARY DISCUSSION
SERIES*

Charles F. Pfeiffer

BAKER BOOK HOUSE
Grand Rapids, Michigan

Introduction

The great leaders of ancient Israel, in company with those of the Christian church, were men "of like nature with ourselves" (James 5:17). The Bible does not hesitate to present them as sinful human beings. This may offend those who declare that positive thinking is the answer to all human ills. Biblical teaching is far more realistic than that. Sin is real and so is Satan. The Christian may have victory over sin, but he will never reach a position in which he is free from temptation. As he looks to the Lord Jesus, he has strength to overcome the evil one. Temptation, however, is a fact of life and the wiles of the devil are real.

The study of Biblical characters has the practical value of helping us see how others reacted in times of temptation. They did not always gain a victory. David's adultery and murder present a sordid picture in the life of a man who is otherwise regarded as one of the great men of Israel. Abraham's lie concerning his relationship to Sarah caused him to leave Egypt in disgrace.

Two major lessons can be gleaned from the sins of these heroes of faith: (1) When we allow our minds and hearts to stray from the Lord, we are capable of committing even the worst of crimes. A history of faithfulness and loyalty does not guarantee that we will continue in the path of God's will. (2) The God of our salvation is a forgiving God. He does not take sin lightly, and sometimes there are consequences of our sins that follow us all our days. God knows the heart, however, and the broken heart He does not despise. There is hope even for a David. The heroes of the Bible may have sinned, but they show us the way back to fellowship with God. Since they are so much like ourselves, we profit spiritually by giving attention to their lives.

CONTENTS

1 ABRAHAM
Friend of God

Abraham is considered to be the natural and spiritual father of Jews and Arabs, as well as the spiritual father of Christians. Judaism, Christianity, and Islam look to him as the man who rejected the idolatry of his day and began an extraordinary pilgrimage of faith. During his lifetime he owned no real estate, except for the burial plot purchased after the death of his wife Sarah, but he believed the promise that one day his descendants would occupy the entire land of Canaan. In a fuller sense he was a sojourner here, looking for "a city that has foundations whose builder and maker is God."

ABRAHAM'S BACKGROUND

Abraham, or Abram as he was first called, was a descendant of Noah's son Shem (Gen. 11:10-32). For this reason he and his descendants are known as Shemites or, as we say today, Semites. We first meet Abraham's family in Ur of the Chaldeans (Gen. 27:28), usually identified with a mound known as al-Muqayyar ("mound of pitch") in southern Iraq near the Euphrates River.

Excavations at al-Muqayyar during the 1920s by C. Leonard Woolley have revealed a Sumerian city of high artistic and cultural attainment which flourished at least five centuries before the time of Abraham. Abraham was heir to a culture which has a tradition of writing going back to around 3200 B.C., a mathematical system based on the number 60, temple architecture, and high artistic accomplishment. We do not know the extent of Abraham's involvement in the life of Ur, but we do know that he broke with its system of polytheism. The Lord, Yahweh, later to be known as the God of Israel, appeared to Abraham, and Abraham obeyed His command (cf. Acts 7:2-4).

ABRAHAM'S JOURNEYS

During Abraham's lifetime he traveled through much of the region known as the Fertile Crescent. From Ur he traveled northwestward following the course of the Euphrates River to the Balikh River, then due northward to Harran (Haran) where he settled for a time. Accompanying him were Sarai (Sarah) his wife, Terah his father, and his nephew Lot. While they were at Haran, Terah died. Then, in obedience to the divine command, Abraham with his wife and his nephew and their servants moved southwestward to Canaan, the land God had promised to Abraham and his descendants.

In Canaan we find Abraham living a semi-nomadic life. He pitches his tents near the cities—Shechem, Bethel, and (later) Hebron—but Abraham is always a stranger and sojourner; for "at that time the Canaanites were in the land" (Gen. 12:6b).

During a period of famine in Canaan, Abraham and his family journeyed to Egypt. There Abraham feared that Pharaoh might want to take the beautiful Sarah for his harem. Sensing possible physical danger to himself, Abraham asked Sarah to pose as his sister rather than his wife. So Pharaoh honored Abraham as Sarah's brother, instead of killing him as the husband of the woman he wanted to marry. Abraham had told a half-truth in stating that Sarah was his sister (see Gen. 20:12), but the intention to deceive was clear. The Bible does not hesitate to declare the sins of its heroes. When things began to go wrong in Pharaoh's household, the Egyptian ruler rightly concluded that his conduct toward Sarah was responsible for the calamities that befell him. Pharaoh returned Sarah to Abraham, and ordered them to leave Egypt.

Back in the Negev region of southern Canaan we find that Abraham and Lot are both prospering. At this point problems began to arise between the herdsmen of the two men, with the result that Abraham concluded that he and his nephew should separate. Generously, Abraham gave Lot his choice of the region most suitable for his manner of life. Lot chose what appeared to be the best region—the well-watered Jordan Valley in the neighborhood of Sodom. Abraham was left with what appeared to be the less desirable land of Canaan and we find him in the Hebron region.

Lot's fortunes became more and more identified with Sodom. When a confederation of kings from the East attacked Sodom and its allies they took Lot captive along with other inhabitants of the city and much booty. Abraham learned what had happened and immediately organized a rescue party of 318 men. The result was that he surprised the kings of the East, defeated them in battle, set free the captives, and reclaimed the booty.

On his way home, Abraham met Melchizedek, the priest-king of Salem (Jerusalem). Melchizedek blessed Abraham, and Abraham paid tithes to Melchizedek. We are reminded in this incident that there were others besides Abraham who worshiped the true God. This ancient priest, living long before the Levitical priesthood in Israel, was considered a type and forerunner of the Messiah (cf. Ps. 110:4; Heb. 7:1-17).

GOD'S PROMISES

Abraham, the man of faith, believes God. Faith has its object in the revealed will of God. This promise is first stated in Genesis 12:2-3. There God promises: A land—to be occupied by Abraham's descendants; A great nation—to be comprised of Abraham's descendants; A blessed people—a nation blessed by God and mediating God's blessings to others.

This blessing is both particularistic and universalistic. Particularism is seen in the choice of one man (nation), the object of God's special care. Others will be judged by their attitude toward this chosen people (Gen. 12:3a). Yet there is a universalistic note. Israel will be the means through which blessing reaches all mankind. God's love will reach "all the families of the earth" (Gen. 12:3b).

God's promises are repeated and amplified at critical moments in Abraham's career. After Lot chooses the best of the land for himself, God asks Abraham to look toward the north, south, east, and west, with the assurance that "all the land which you see I will give to you and to your descendants for ever" (Gen. 13:15).

After returning from the rescue of Lot, Abraham refused any of the spoil which he might properly have claimed. He did not want the king of Sodom to say, "I have made Abram rich" (Gen. 14:23). Then the Lord said, "Fear not, Abram, I am your shield; your reward shall be very great" (Gen. 15:1).

THE PROBLEM OF AN HEIR

When God spoke of His blessings to Abraham, Abraham replied, "O Lord God, what wilt thou give me, for I continue childless, and the heir of my house is Eliezer of Damascus?" (Gen. 15:2). It was customary for men who had no sons of their own to adopt a favorite servant. In this way the man would be cared for in his old age, and proper funerary rites provided at the time of death. In the absence of a natural son, the adopted son would be heir. Abraham seems to have adopted Eliezer. God spoke of blessing, but Abraham had no natural son, and so the promises seemed meaningless. God replied by assuring Abraham that his own natural son would be his heir, and that his descendants would be as numberless as the stars of heaven (Gen. 15:1-6).

As years went by and Sarah did not bear a child she urged Abraham to take her Egyptian slave girl Hagar and father a child by her (Gen. 16:1-9). In this way Abraham became the father of Ishmael, who would have a history and inherit blessings uniquely his. Ishmael was not the promised heir, however (Gen. 16:7-15).

Abraham was pleased with Ishmael and would have been content to have him as his heir, but again God intervened. God renewed the covenant with Abraham and instituted the rite of circumcision as the covenant sign (Gen. 17:1-15). Abraham's wife, Sarah, well beyond the normal time of childbearing, would become the mother of the child of promise—Isaac. The message was brought to Abraham (and Sarah) by strangers, to whom Abraham showed the hospitality characteristic of the desert regions (Gen. 18:1-15).

From this time on there was no question that Isaac would be Abraham's heir, but there was one serious test awaiting Abraham. God told Abraham to take his beloved son to the land of Moriah and there on the mount offer Isaac as a burnt offering. In a very moving scene (Gen. 22) we find father and son preparing for a sacrifice. The son does not know what the sacrifice is to be, but the father says, "God will provide himself the lamb for a burnt offering, my son" (Gen. 22:8). Finally the altar is prepared and Isaac bound. At the last minute, as Abraham has shown that he would obey God even in killing his son, God intervenes: "Do not lay your hand on the lad. . ." (Gen. 22:12). A ram caught in the thicket would be an acceptable substitute, and Isaac goes free. Human sacrifice, common among Israel's neighbors, would not become part of the faith of Israel.

The career of Abraham was almost ended by the time of Isaac's birth. Death came to Sarah at Hebron when she was 127, and here Abraham bargained for and purchased a burial place from a local land owner, Ephron the Hittite (Gen. 23:7-16). The cave of Machpelah, as it was called, was not only the burial place of Sarah, but subsequently Abraham (Gen. 25:9-10), Isaac (Gen. 35:29), Rebekah (Gen. 49:31), Leah (Gen. 49:31), and Jacob (Gen. 50:13) were buried there.

After Sarah's death, Abraham sent his servant, perhaps Eliezer of Damascus, to the region around Haran, "the city of Nahor," to secure a proper bride for Isaac. Marriage must not be contracted with the idolatrous Canaanites but with the patriarchal family in upper Mesopotamia. There the servant met the fair Rebekah who offered to provide water for him and his camels—a sign that God had prospered his journey. Rebekah expressed her willingness to go with Abraham's servant, and she became Isaac's wife.

Abraham had another wife, Keturah, in his old age. He had additional sons, and he provided generously for them, but Isaac was the chief heir (Gen. 25:1-6). Abraham lived to be 175, and his sons Isaac and Ishmael were present to bury him beside Sarah in the cave of Machpelah.

QUESTIONS

1. In what sense is Abraham the father of Christians?

2. The Jews are sometimes called "the chosen people." Is this a Biblical description? Chosen for what?

3. In a time of famine, Abraham traveled to Egypt. Was that journey an evidence of lack of faith in God's ability to provide for him in Canaan?

4. Lot's move in the direction of Sodom proved very unwise. Could Lot have anticipated the troubles that came to him there?

5. Abraham considered Melchizedek to be a priest of the true God. What was the source of Melchizedek's faith?

6. On what grounds did Sarah offer her slave girl Hagar to Abraham as a secondary wife? Can this practice be Biblically justified?

2 JACOB
Man with a New Name

The story of Jacob is the story of two nations—their rivalries and their ultimate decision to live in peace. The promises made to Abraham were transmitted to Isaac and then to Jacob. Jacob, however, was not Isaac's firstborn son. His twin brother Esau was the elder (Gen. 25:25). Why Jacob received the blessing instead of Esau is the subject of three stories in the Book of Genesis.

The first story concerns the birth of the boys. Rebekah experienced considerable difficulty during her pregnancy, and she became aware that she was bearing twins when the Lord gave her this oracle: "Two nations are in your womb, and two peoples, born of you, shall be divided; The one shall be stronger than the other, the elder shall serve the younger" (Gen. 25:23).

When the twins were born, the first was red in color—hence the name Edom, and hairy—hence the name Esau. The names are often used interchangeably; but Esau is usually the name of the man, Edom the name of the people, and Edomites the name of his descendants. The second child was named Jacob, the supplanter, the cheat. At birth he grabbed Esau's heel as if to pull him back and attempt to get ahead of him.

As the boys grew up they showed opposite characteristics. Esau was a hunter who loved the out-of-doors. His father was particularly fond of him. Jacob, on the other hand, was a quiet lad who preferred to stay in the tents; and he became the darling of his mother.

A second story relates the account of Esau returning home famished after a hard day in the fields. Jacob, characteristically, was boiling pottage (a kind of stew) when Esau appeared and asked for food. Jacob, taking advantage of his brother's hunger, asked Esau to sell his birthright. Esau reasoned that the birthright would be meaningless to him if he died of starvation; so he sold his birthright. He ate and was satisfied (Gen. 25:27-34). While we might question the conduct of both brothers, it is significant that judgment is placed primarily on Esau: "Thus Esau despised his birthright" (Gen. 25:34b). Esau was a secular man. He could not trust God in his hour of need. His birthright could be surrendered in exchange for a "mess of pottage."

The third story relates events shortly before the death of Isaac. The father still planned to give his principal blessing to his favored son, Esau. Isaac asked Esau to go out to the fields and hunt game which would be cooked as the meal to be eaten preparatory to the utterance of the blessing. We know from the Nuzi tablets, discovered in the 1920s near Kirkuk in Iraq, that such blessings were considered valid and binding in courts of law.

Rebekah, however, was determined that the blessing should go to her favorite, Jacob. She contrived an elaborate act of deception. She asked Jacob to bring two kids from the flock to cook in place of the game Esau was hunting. Rebekah brought some of Esau's garments and placed them on Jacob so he would have the smell of Esau. She took the skins of the kids and placed them on the smooth part of Jacob's neck, in order that Isaac would feel the hair and think he was touching his favorite son, Esau.

When Jacob appeared before his blind father to get the blessing intended for Esau the deception was complete. Jacob assured his father that he had returned from the hunt so quickly because of the blessing of the Lord. But Isaac was suspicious, and so he asked that his son come near. Isaac felt Jacob, but the hairy covering used as a disguise fooled him. The sense of smell and touch convinced him that it was Esau who had come for the blessing. The sound of the voice constituted a problem (Gen. 27:22), but the other senses convinced him that he was right in uttering the intended blessing.

The blessing was vast in scope. Jacob would enjoy the dew of heaven and the fatness of the earth. He would be in a land which would produce abundance of grain and wine (Gen. 27:28). Politically Jacob (=Israel) would have its sovereignty recognized by many peoples, and even his brothers (including Esau) would be subject to him (Gen. 28:29).

As could be expected, Esau returned from the hunt only to learn that his father had already given the blessing to Jacob. In modern concepts of law the deception would have nullified the blessing and Isaac's words to Jacob would be considered void. In ancient Israelite thought, however, the word itself was deemed sacred and it had to be considered valid no matter what the circumstances under which it was given. Isaac could not go back on his word to Jacob even though Esau pleaded for a blessing.

The blessing given to Esau seemed more of a curse than a blessing. He would live away from the fatness of the earth—that is, in the waste places of Edom. He would be a fighter, living by his sword. Esau would serve Jacob—or, translated into nationalistic terms, the Edomites would be subject to the Israelites. On the other hand, one day Esau-Edom would be free from bondage to Jacob-Israel. That was the one ray of hope in the otherwise dismal blessing (Gen. 27:39-40).

Since Isaac would soon be dead, Esau decided to bide his time. After Isaac's death, Esau would kill Jacob and thus avenge the wrong which he felt had been committed. However, Rebekah again intervened. She decided that Jacob must leave the country for his own good. At the same time Rebekah was convinced that Jacob must marry someone from her homeland in northern Mesopotamia. Esau had married local Canaanite girls, and this was an occasion of grief to both Isaac and Rebekah.

THE JOURNEY TO PADDAN-ARAM

With Isaac's blessing, Jacob began the long journey northward in the direction of Haran. One night he slept with a stone for a pillow and dreamed of a ladder reaching from earth to heaven. Angels were ascending and descending the ladder, and God revealed Himself to Jacob from its summit. God identified Himself as the God of Abraham and of Isaac. In words reminiscent of God's promise to Abraham, Jacob was told that his descendants would be like the dust of the earth. They would occupy the land to the north, south, east, and west of the place where he was then resting. All the families of the earth would be blessed through them. God would be with Jacob in his journey northward, and would one day bring him back.

When Jacob awoke he called the place of his dream Beth-el, "the house of God." He vowed that if the Lord would prosper his way and bring him back safely, he would worship the Lord at the pillar he had set up and give to the Lord a tenth of his possessions (Gen. 28:18-22).

Jacob arrived in the vicinity of Haran and soon caught a glimpse of Rachel, the daughter of Laban, tending her father's sheep. It was love at first sight. When Laban suggested that Jacob work for him, Jacob offered to work seven years for Laban's younger daughter, the beautiful Rachel (Gen. 29:18).

The years sped by, and the time came for Jacob to claim his bride. Imagine his consternation when he found that Laban had given him Leah, the older and less beautiful daughter, instead of Rachel. When confronted with this breach of contract, Laban protested that the custom of the land demanded that the older daughters be married first. Jacob, however, could have Rachel also—in exchange for seven more years of labor.

In all, Jacob stayed twenty years with Laban, paying for his two wives and the cattle he accumulated. The first of Jacob's sons were born to Leah, and Rachel was unhappy that she could bear no children. As Sarah had done earlier when she bore no children to Abraham, Rachel offered her maid Bilhah with the thought that she might have children which would be accounted to herself. Ancient marriage contracts stipulated that a childless wife is obligated to provide a substitute who will bear children for her husband; so Sarah and Rachel were both observing this ancient custom. In all, Jacob had twelve sons, children of these four mothers: Leah, Rachel, Leah's servant girl, and Rachel's servant girl.

The line of promise continued from Abraham to Isaac and from Isaac to Jacob (=Israel). From Jacob, however, it does not go to just one individual, but to all the sons or tribes of Israel. Graphically we might suggest:

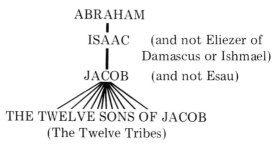

ABRAHAM

ISAAC   (and not Eliezer of Damascus or Ishmael)

JACOB   (and not Esau)

THE TWELVE SONS OF JACOB
(The Twelve Tribes)

After twenty years with Laban, Jacob sensed a growing friction. Laban now had sons who were jealous of Jacob, and Laban himself was no longer friendly. It may be that Laban had adopted Jacob as his heir before his own sons were born. When this happens, natural sons take precedence over adopted sons; so Jacob would no longer have the honored position he had formerly enjoyed.

Jacob began to assemble his wives, children, and livestock, and then started homeward toward Canaan without consulting Laban. When Laban learned what had happened he pursued Jacob, caught up with him, and scolded him for leaving secretly. He also charged Jacob with stealing his household gods (Gen. 31:30). The possession of the household gods (*terephim*) was considered the right of the chief heir. Rachel took them, perhaps with the thought of keeping her husband instead of one of her brothers as Laban's chief heir. She did not tell Jacob what she had done, and Laban did not find them when he searched the camp. Jacob was angered at Laban's false (as far as Jacob knew) accusation, but the two decided to part on amicable terms.

After the encounter with Laban, another encounter could be anticipated—with Esau. Would Esau still be angry with Jacob? Had he given up his plan to kill him? These must have been problems that disturbed Jacob as he neared Esau's territory.

Before meeting Esau, however, Jacob had yet another encounter. He had reached the Jabbok and was in the process of fording the stream with his wives, children, and possessions. When his caravan was safely on the southern bank, Jacob was making the final check, alone, on the northern bank. There he met a mysterious assailant who wrestled with him all night. This "man" humbled Jacob, putting his thigh out of joint. At daybreak the assailant wanted to leave, but Jacob insisted that He first give a blessing. The one who could humble could also help. The assailant gave Jacob a new name. Jacob would now be called Israel, the one who strives with God and men, and prevails (Gen. 32:28). Jacob was convinced that this was no mere mortal who had wrestled with him. Jacob had seen God, and he called the place Peniel ("The face of God"). The cheater, the supplanter (Jacob) was now the victorious one. God had humbled Jacob; Jacob had been blessed by God.

The encounter with Esau was somewhat of an anticlimax. Twenty years had brought changes to both brothers. Each had been blessed with family and possessions. Old quarrels were forgotten. The result was that Esau returned to Mount Seir, his home, and Jacob moved on toward Canaan.

The return to Canaan brought its own problems. Shechem, a Hivite prince in the land, raped Dinah, Leah's daughter, and so her brothers determined revenge. They persuaded the Hivites to become circumcised, like the Israelites; then while they were recovering, Simeon and Levi, sons of Jacob, staged an invasion, killing all the males and plundering the city. Movable property, including women and livestock, was captured as prey. Jacob reprimanded Simeon and Levi, reminding them that the Israelites were few in number and that they could not hope to stand against all the inhabitants of the land of Canaan.

Jacob began the return journey to Bethel, where he had seen God at the top of the ladder on his flight twenty years before. First of all he made the Israelites abandon the foreign gods they had accumulated (Gen. 35:2); then, at Bethel, God renewed the covenant earlier made with Jacob. Jacob set up a pillar there as a memorial of the faithfulness of God and His promises (Gen. 35:14).

Soon after these events Rachel, Jacob's favorite wife, died in giving birth to her second son, Benjamin (Gen. 35:16-21). The beloved Rachel had earlier borne Joseph. After her death, Jacob continued to show his love for Rachel in his favoritism toward Joseph and Benjamin.

Jacob's favoritism toward Joseph was seen in the special coat given to him which marked him out as one preferred above his brothers. Joseph's dreams of preeminence also caused the brothers to be jealous, to the point where they determined to kill him. Providentially, this was not done, but Joseph was sold into slavery in Egypt. Jacob, however, was convinced by his older sons that Joseph had died at the hand of wild beasts.

There is an irony in Jacob's later life. He had deceived his father decades before; now his sons deceive him. His favorite wife is dead, and now (so he thinks) the oldest son of Rachel is dead also. Benjamin, the surviving son, now takes the chief place in the father's heart; but his brothers are more tolerant of the father's favoritism toward Benjamin than they were over favoritism toward Joseph. Perhaps they had grown a bit older and wiser themselves.

Joseph, of course, was alive in Egypt where he had been honored as vizier, second only to Pharaoh in authority. After Joseph revealed himself to his brothers, they brought the news back to Jacob, who naturally could scarcely believe the report. Jacob and his sons went down to Egypt where they were honored as Joseph's family. Jacob died in Egypt at the age of 147 (Gen. 47:28), but his body was taken to the ancestral burying place at Hebron.

QUESTIONS

1. The problem of parental favoritism is evident throughout the stories of Jacob and Esau. Must parents treat all children alike? Is favoritism ever justifiable?

2. What defects in character do we find in Esau?

3. Jacob's encounter on the banks of the Jabbok had a profound influence on his life. Are there comparable experiences today? in your own life? in the lives of others?

4. Among the patriarchs it was considered desirable to marry someone from the home area rather than local Canaanite girls. Why? Is this a form of racism? religious intolerance?

5. Romantic love dominates the story of Jacob and Rachel. Was romantic love rare in antiquity? Are there other Biblical examples?

3 JOSEPH
Slave Who Became Prime Minister

Joseph had everything going for him. As the first son of his father's favorite wife, from birth on he enjoyed a favored position. We would probably say that he was spoiled but, interestingly, the Bible does not speak of any sins of Joseph. He is the Biblical example of a young man who remains faithful in the midst of adversity. Joseph may have brought on some of his troubles, but it is his faithfulness to God under all circumstances that we are asked to remember.

We know nothing of Joseph's childhood. His mother, Rachel, had wanted a son. Children had been born to Leah, Jacob's other wife, to Rachel's maid Bilhah, and to Leah's maid Zilpah (Gen. 30:1-12). Rachel felt herself a failure as a wife until "God remembered Rachel, and God hearkened to her and opened her womb" (Gen.

30:22). Rejoicing at the birth of Joseph, Rachel said, "God has taken away my reproach" (Gen. 30:23).

Joseph was born while Jacob was with Laban in Paddan-aram, but Jacob and his household moved southward toward Canaan shortly afterward. We next read of Joseph as he is shepherding his father's flocks with his brothers at the age of seventeen (Gen. 37:2). Joseph was not getting along with his brothers. When he had opportunity he reported to Jacob their misconduct (Gen. 37:2b), and his father openly favored Joseph. The special coat (Gen. 37:3) given Joseph by Jacob must have been particularly offensive. It seemed to shout out to the rest of the family, "Joseph is the favorite! Joseph is the favorite!"

Joseph did not improve matters by telling of his dreams. There was nothing mysterious in the dreams. The sheaves of the brothers bowed down to Joseph's sheaf! The sun, moon, and eleven stars bowed down to Joseph (Gen. 37:5-9). This was too much even for Jacob: "What is this dream that you have dreamed? Shall I and your mother and your brothers indeed come to bow ourselves to the ground before you?" (Gen. 37:10). On the surface we seem to be observing a spoiled boy with dreams of grandeur. In the light of what follows, we must see more than that. Indeed, Joseph's brothers will bow down to him in Egypt as they come seeking food in a time of famine. For the moment neither Joseph, nor his parents, nor his brothers know how this dream will find fulfillment. But God is keeping watch over His own.

God's purposes are not always known to men, and the way they are realized often comes as a surprise. Joseph's brothers were jealous of him, and they determined to kill him when opportunity came. Opportunity came rather soon, for Jacob sent Joseph to a far distant area to check on the welfare of his brothers as they were tending the flocks. When his brothers saw him coming, they plotted to kill Joseph. "Here comes this dreamer," they said. They would rid themselves of him once and for all. They would kill him, cast his body into a pit, and tell Jacob that a wild beast had devoured him. Then his dreams would be proved meaningless (Gen. 37:18-20).

Reuben, the oldest son, felt a sense of responsibility for Joseph. He suggested that they cast him into a pit alive. Bloodshed is a serious crime, and Reuben persuaded them to abandon their plans for murder. Before Reuben could get back to deliver Joseph from the pit, however, his brothers found a new means of ridding themselves of him. Traders en route to Egypt passed by, and they decided to sell Joseph into slavery. The rest of the plan for deceiving their father was then carried out. They dipped Joseph's robe in the blood of a goat and took it to Jacob, claiming they had unexpectedly discovered it. Jacob was convinced that Joseph was dead.

Joseph's life in Egypt illustrates the psalmist's statement about the righteous man: "In all that he does, he prospers" (Ps. 1:3). Joseph became a slave in the household of Potiphar, an Egyptian official (Gen. 39:1). Even in this menial position, Joseph honored God and God was with

Joseph. A popular proverb says, "You can't keep a good man down." Potiphar, an officer of Pharaoh, soon observed that Joseph was an unusual slave. He could be trusted under all circumstances. Potiphar made Joseph his majordomo, overseer of all his possessions (Gen. 39:2-6). Joseph found a place of service, and Potiphar prospered. For the moment it appeared that Joseph had a good job for the rest of his life.

At that point Potiphar's wife entered the story, and Joseph's situation was radically altered. Mrs. Potiphar was physically attracted to Joseph, but he would not yield to her. One day she grabbed his outer garment as she demanded that Joseph have sexual relations with her (Gen. 39:12). Joseph fled, leaving the garment in her hand. He would not sin against his God or violate his master's trust (Gen. 39:8-9).

The events that follow should serve as a warning that things are not always as they appear. A vicious person can malign another and use circumstantial evidence to bring a false accusation. Joseph's garment was all Potiphar's wife needed, for here was evidence that Joseph had attacked her. She would only have to say that she cried out for help, and he—the guilty one—fled leaving the garment with her. What more evidence would be needed?

Joseph the honored majordomo becomes Joseph the prisoner. He is no longer the trusted servant. Now he is in jail where the king's prisoners were confined (Gen. 39:20). Yet even in prison, Joseph prospered. The keeper of the prison trusted Joseph and soon Joseph was given a position of responsibility comparable to what he had in Potiphar's household (Gen. 39:21-23).

In his years with his brothers in Canaan, Joseph had been called a dreamer. In prison we see him as an interpreter of dreams. Two of Pharaoh's officers had been jailed because of an unnamed offense against the king. They dreamed dreams which puzzled them. The chief butler saw in his dream a vine with branches and clusters which ripened into grapes. He pressed the grapes into Pharaoh's cup and placed the cup in Pharaoh's hand (Gen. 40:9-11). Joseph interpreted the dream: Within three days Pharaoh would restore the chief butler to his former position. Pharaoh would lift up the butler's head—that is, he would change his sorrow into joy as he assigned him his former responsibilities. Joseph asked that the chief butler remember him and intercede with Pharaoh to effect his release from prison (Gen. 40:9-15).

The chief baker was impressed with the interpretation of the chief butler's dream, and so he told his own dream to Joseph. In his dream he saw three baskets of cakes on his head. Baked food for Pharaoh was in the top basket, but birds were eating it from the basket. Joseph's interpretation was not a good one. Within three days the chief baker would be beheaded and hanged on a tree and the birds would eat his flesh.

The interpretations of the two dreams have an interesting play on words. The chief butler's head would be lifted up (Gen. 40:13). He would no longer be downcast but could lift his head with joy. The chief baker's head would be lifted up—from him (Gen. 40:19). He would be beheaded! The idea of birds eating his flesh would be particularly repulsive to an Egyptian. Great pains were taken in the mummification of bodies to preserve their identity into the next life.

Joseph's interpretations proved correct (Gen. 40:20-23). The chief butler was restored and the chief baker was hanged. Sad to say, the chief butler did not remember Joseph; and two years went by before we read of him again. In every generation innocent people suffer, and Joseph's years in prison are a reminder that righteous people may be falsely accused and suffer as a result. We know that Joseph was finally vindicated. It would be interesting to know what his thoughts were as month after month he was confined to prison for a crime of which he was innocent.

Help finally came as a result of more dreams—this time Pharaoh's. The king saw seven fat cows coming from the Nile and feeding on the reed grass along its banks. Then he saw seven lean cows come up and eat the fat cows. In the second dream he saw seven good ears of grain which were swallowed up by seven thin, blighted ears (Gen. 41:1-7). When none of the wise men of Egypt could interpret Pharaoh's dream, the chief butler remembered Joseph's ability in this area. Straightway Pharaoh sent for Joseph to interpret his dream.

Before appearing before Pharaoh, Joseph shaved himself and changed his clothes. Semites were bearded; Egyptians were clean shaven. As a courtesy, Joseph shaved for his audience with Pharaoh.

Joseph made it clear that he had no wisdom in himself. He prefaced his interpretation with the comment, "It is not in me; God will give Pharaoh a favorable answer" (Gen. 41:16). The God of Israel was concerned about Egypt. In mercy He was speaking through Joseph to Pharaoh, telling the Egyptian king that years of plenty would be followed by years of famine (Gen. 41:26-36). The Egyptians should conserve food during the seven bountiful years so that they would have enough during the seven years of famine.

Pharaoh saw in Joseph the man he needed to lead Egypt during the crisis period ahead. Joseph became vizier, or prime minister. He had the king's signet ring, so he could issue decrees in the king's name and seal them with the king's seal. His prison garments were put aside and he wore fine linen, with a gold chain around his neck. People were asked to do homage to Joseph as he rode the second chariot in the land. Only Pharaoh himself received greater honor.

Joseph was given an Egyptian name, Zaphenath-paneah, and an Egyptian wife called Asenath, daughter of Potiphera, priest of On, modern Heliopolis. At the age of thirty Joseph had survived the jealousy of his brothers and the hatred of Potiphar's wife. His period in jail was over and now he was an Egyptian official with total power over the economy of the land (Gen. 41:44). During the years of plenty Asenath bore two sons to Joseph: Ephraim and Manasseh.

After the years of plenty, famine became widespread throughout the Near East. Egypt, thanks to Joseph's wise policy of conservation, had food enough during the difficult years, and other peoples found they could buy food in Egypt when local supplies were exhausted. It was under these circumstances that Joseph again met his brothers from Canaan.

Jacob, now an old man, sent ten of Joseph's brothers to buy food in Egypt. Benjamin, the only surviving son of Rachel (as far as Jacob knew), stayed home with his father. Benjamin had become the father's favorite after Joseph's supposed death, but a change in the other sons of Jacob is noticeable. They had been jealous of Joseph, but now they are willing to indulge their father in his favoritism toward Benjamin.

When the brothers reached Egypt they were sent to Joseph. They did not recognize him in his Egyptian attire and in the splendor of the Egyptian court, but he recognized them. Joseph spoke roughly to them, accusing them of being spies. In defense they told the story of their lives. They were twelve brothers. The youngest is at home with their father, and one "is no more" (Gen. 42:13). Joseph now determined to be reunited with Benjamin, the son of both Jacob and Rachel, his only full brother. He continued to accuse the ten of being spies. He kept them in prison for a time, then held Simeon as a hostage and let the others return to Canaan with orders to bring back Benjamin. Joseph spoke to them through an interpreter, although he understood all they said among themselves.

Joseph gave orders that the bags of his brothers be filled with grain, and he replaced the money of each of them in their sacks. Jacob was grief stricken when his sons returned without

Simeon and with the demand that Benjamin be sent to Egypt (Gen. 42:36). Reuben, again taking responsibility as the firstborn, promised to bring Benjamin back: "Slay my two sons if I do not bring him back to you; put him in my hands, and I will bring him back to you" (Gen. 42:37).

With great reluctance, Jacob allowed his sons to take a second journey to Egypt, this time with Benjamin. They brought double the needed money, to make up for the money found in the sacks on their return from Egypt. They brought down a present for the Egyptian vizier, "a little balm and a little honey, gum, myrrh, pistachio nuts, and almonds" (Gen. 43:11).

Joseph was so overwhelmed with emotion that he almost gave himself away when he saw Benjamin with his half-brothers (Gen. 43:30). Joseph devised a plan to keep Benjamin with him in Egypt. After treating them all to a royal banquet, he commanded his steward to fill the sacks of each of the men with grain, to replace the money in the sacks, and to put Joseph's silver cup in Benjamin's sack. The plan was a simple one. The brothers would be charged with the theft of the cup. Their sacks would be searched and the cup found in Benjamin's sack. Joseph then would detain Benjamin, identify himself to him, and keep him in Egypt as his own brother.

Things did not work out exactly as planned, however. Joseph's men overtook the brothers, searched the entire caravan, and found the cup in Benjamin's sack. So far, so good. When Joseph attempted to detain Benjamin, Judah intervened. He eloquently pleaded for the release of Benjamin. Jacob had never recovered from the loss of Joseph. To add the loss of Benjamin, the sole remaining son of his wife Rachel, would kill Jacob. Judah offered to stay himself in place of Benjamin. Jacob could get along without Judah, but the loss of Benjamin would surely kill him (Gen. 44:13-34).

This was too much for Joseph. In a tear-filled scene he identified himself to his brothers: "I am your brother Joseph whom you sold into Egypt" (Gen. 45:4). True, they had sold him into Egypt, but God had overruled all things. God brought Joseph to Egypt in order to save life. Two years of famine were past, but five more were ahead. They must return to Canaan, report Joseph's honored position to Jacob, and return with Jacob to Egypt where Joseph can provide for them.

God told Jacob that he should go to Egypt. He would see his beloved Joseph, and at death Joseph's hand would close his eyes (Gen. 46:4). Counting children and grandchildren, there were seventy of the household of Jacob that moved to Egypt and settled in the land of Goshen in the eastern delta region (Gen. 46:27-28). The Pharaoh of Joseph's time was favorable to Joseph and his family. While Joseph's policies may have seemed severe (see Gen. 47:13-26), the Egyptians were grateful to him for saving their lives (Gen. 47:25).

Jacob lived seventeen years in Egypt (Gen. 47:28) before his death. He showed his love for Joseph by adopting Ephraim and Manasseh (Gen. 48:5-20), Joseph's sons. For this reason, later the nation of Israel did not have a single tribe of Joseph, but two Joseph tribes—Ephraim and Manasseh. In his blessing on Joseph, Jacob spoke of him as a fruitful bough by a spring with branches running over the wall. The fruit of Joseph's life had been the blessing of his own family, and blessings on the Egyptians as well. He had been attacked and harassed, but the God of Jacob gave strength and blessing throughout his life (Gen. 49:22-26).

After Jacob's death, Joseph's brothers feared that he might seek revenge for their treatment of him when he was a youth. Joseph, however, said to them, "As for you, you meant evil against me; but God meant it for good, to bring it about that many people should be kept alive, as they are today" (Gen. 50:15-21). Man is responsible for his acts, but a sovereign God works out His purposes even through the sinful deeds of wicked men. Joseph's brothers did not thwart God's will, they brought about its accomplishment. So today with us: it may help us to forgive those who wrong us if we take the long view of God's good and acceptable and perfect will.

Joseph's life span was 110 years—the ideal life according to Egyptian thought. Before his death he asked his brothers to vow that they would take his remains with them at the time of the Exodus from Egypt (Gen. 50:25-26). For the moment, the descendants of Jacob, the Israelites, were well treated in Egypt; but it was God's will that they one day return to the land of promise. That came about when a new dynasty, unfriendly to foreigners, came into power. When Israel left Egypt under Moses, Joseph's remains were taken along and given permanent burial in Canaan. According to Egyptian custom, Joseph was embalmed. His mummified remains served as a prophecy that the promises made to Abraham, Isaac, and Jacob were valid, and that one day Canaan would be the home of the Israelites.

QUESTIONS

1. Why was Joseph his father's favorite?

2. How did Joseph aggravate his problems? How could he have improved his attitude and actions toward his brothers?

3. Was Joseph right in the way he treated his brothers when they came to him for food in Egypt?

4. What was Joseph's view of divine providence? Did he accept his sufferings as the will of God for him?

5. Evaluate Joseph's economic measures in Egypt. Did they help the Egyptians? Did they increase the power of the government?

6. Joseph married an Egyptian. Does this run counter to what Abraham and Isaac desired for their children?

4 MOSES
Lawgiver

Moses was born during critical times for the Israelites. Egypt had been ruled by a dynasty that was understandably antiforeign. Semites from the East known as Hyksos had taken power in Egypt, with the result that native born Egyptians felt humiliated by foreign rule. But now a native dynasty was again in control, and foreigners were out of favor.

Joseph had been a foreigner whose service to the Egyptian people was recognized by all. Naturally, this new dynasty "did not know Joseph" (Exod. 1:8). They forgot the service he had done for Egypt, and they reduced his descendants to the status of slaves. They greatly feared that the Israelites would sympathize with potential invaders (Exod. 1:10).

Logically we might assume that Egypt would be glad to get rid of the Israelites. Slave labor, however, was useful in Pharaoh's building projects (Exod. 1:11). The problem was to get work out of the Israelites without allowing them to become strong enough to threaten Egyptian security.

We read successively of three attempts at population control. The first was one of oppressive labor conditions. Taskmasters would demand unreasonable work loads of the Israelite slaves. Pharaoh's store cities Pithom and Raamses must be built in record time! To quote an old proverb (only partially true), "Hard work never killed anyone." Of these slaves we read, "But the more they were oppressed, the more they multiplied and the more they spread abroad" (Exod. 1:12). Cruel taskmasters might make the Israelites serve "with rigor" but the spirit of the people was not broken.

Second, the Egyptian ruler decided to work through the midwives. The midwife will be responsible for killing all male infants of the Hebrews. Murder is a serious crime, however; and we say to the credit of the midwives that they would not obey the king's barbarous order. There may even have been some truth in the midwives' excuse: "The Hebrew women are not like the Egyptian women; for they are vigorous and are delivered before the midwife comes to them" (Exod. 1:19). Cultured, sheltered Egyptian women may have been less ready for childbirth than the slave population of Israelites.

When neither oppressive labor nor the orders to the midwives cut down on the number of surviving male babies, Pharaoh issued direct orders to all his people: "Every son that is born to the Hebrews you shall cast into the Nile, but you shall let every daughter live" (Exod. 1:22). The intention was clear: death by drowning for all Israelite male children.

We read, however, of the birth of a son to a family of the tribe of Levi. He is placed in the Nile, in a basket made of bulrushes and daubed with bitumen and pitch (Exod. 2:3). The boy's sister is watching nearby to take advantage of any opportunity to save the child. Pharaoh's orders are carried out—the boy is in the river! Pharaoh's daughter approaches. Her heart goes out to the infant, and she accepts the suggestion of the child's sister that she employ a Hebrew nurse to care for the foundling. What irony! Pharaoh's daughter will pay Moses' mother to care for her own child! He who was doomed to death by the king's decree will grow to manhood in the royal palace! From the Biblical viewpoint, these are not accidents. God is watching over His people in their time of distress.

We have no details concerning the childhood of Moses. We know that he spent his earliest years with his mother, where he must have learned about his background as an Israelite. We know that he was brought to Pharaoh's daughter (Exod. 2:10) where he was educated as a prince in the Egyptian court. Perhaps he was educated with princes from foreign courts, many of whom came to Egypt to get the best available education of the day. The name Moses (Heb. *Mosheh*) may be derived from the Hebrew word meaning "to draw out." We read that Pharaoh's daughter gave her adopted son the name Moses "because I drew him out of the water" (Exod. 2:10). The

Egyptian suffix -mose appears in many royal names: Ah-mose, Thut-mose, Ra-mose, Ka-mose. It means "one who is born of," or "a child of." Thus Ra-mose (often Anglicized Rameses) means "a child of the sun god (Ra)." If Moses had been an Egyptian, he would probably have had the name of an Egyptian god as a prefix to his name.

As the adopted son of Pharaoh's daughter, Moses might have been in line for the throne. Moses, however, chose to identify with his oppressed people. On one occasion he saw an Egyptian taskmaster beating a Hebrew. Springing to the defense of the oppressed Israelite, Moses killed the Egyptian (Exod. 2:11-12). The next day, in attempting to resolve a problem among his own people, Moses learned that he had been seen the day before when he killed the Egyptian. Moses was now considered an enemy of the Egyptians. He fled into the Sinai wilderness where he was welcomed by the nomadic Midianites.

Moses' experiences in Midian comprise the second period of his life. There he was hospitably received by a priest named Reuel, or Jethro (Exod. 2:18; 3:1), after Moses had defended his daughters from attack. Moses married Zipporah, a daughter of Jethro, and in due time their first son, Gershom, was born.

The relationship of Moses to Jethro is comparable to that of Abraham with Melchizedek. In both instances we have Biblical heroes, worshipers of the true God, who acknowledge the validity of the worship of those not in the Biblical line of promise. We may conclude that, while idolatry was rampant in all lands, there were those who knew and worshiped the Lord, and that their faith was comparable to that of the Biblical heroes in the line of Abraham.

The Israelites in slavery in Egypt continued to cry to the Lord for deliverance. Finally God's time had come, and He appeared to Moses in the wilderness. Moses' attention was secured when he saw a mysterious bush which was burning but not consumed (Exod. 3:2). Normally the desert bushes are dry, and they would burn up in an instant if set afire. Moses turned aside to see what was going on. He heard the voice of God, identifying Himself as the God of Abraham, the God of Isaac, and the God of Jacob. God had heard the cry of His people in Egypt and He was sending Moses back to Egypt to lead them to freedom.

Moses was concerned with a practical question. There were many gods in Egypt. How could Moses identify the God who had commissioned him to lead the people to freedom? God identified Himself as the God whose name is "I am who I am," the Hebrew name being Yahweh, or "the Lord" in many versions of the Bible. Yahweh is always a personal name. He is the One who brought Israel from Egypt (Exod. 20:1) and entered into covenant relations with His people at Sinai.

As Moses continued to find objections to fulfilling his mission, God met each problem. If Moses feared that the people would not believe him, God gave him a supernatural sign (Exod. 4:1-10). If Moses protested that he was not a man of eloquence, God appointed Aaron his brother as spokesman (Exod. 5:10-17).

The last part of Moses' life is the most important of all. Leaving Jethro in the wilderness, Moses and his family made their way back to Egypt where he had a series of encounters with Pharaoh. To the request, "Let my people go," Pharaoh was consistently hostile. The God of Israel must prove Himself greater than the gods of Egypt. In a series of ten plagues, the gods of Egypt were shown to be powerless. The Nile River itself, the source of water and life for Egypt, became foul and putrid (Exod. 7:18). Other plagues brought frogs, gnats, flies, disease on the cattle, boils, hail, locusts, and thick darkness throughout the land—except among the Israelites. Although on occasion Pharaoh seemed ready to let the Israelites go (Exod. 10:24), he remained unwilling to recognize the power of Israel's God.

The last plague coincides with the Passover and the Exodus from Egypt. The plague was the death of the firstborn in each Egyptian home. The Israelites were told to prepare for the Exodus. A lamb was to be slain and its blood applied to the lintel and the doorposts. The lamb was to be roasted and eaten by the Israelite families with unleavened bread and bitter herbs (Exod. 12:1-13). Judgment would fall on the Egyptian homes, but to the Israelites God said, "The blood shall be a sign for you, upon the houses where you are, and when I see the blood, I will pass over you, and no plague shall fall upon you to destroy you, when I smite the land of Egypt" (Exod. 12:13).

The Passover was Israel's independence day. Pharaoh would never willingly have released his slaves, but with the death of the firstborn in every Egyptian home he had no choice. God gave marching orders to Moses. Israel must not take the direct route to the land of Canaan, "the way of the Land of the Philistines" (Exod. 13:17), because Israel was not yet ready for warfare. About the time Israel was leaving Egypt, Philistines were being pressured to leave Crete and the Aegean Islands which had been their home. A generation later the Israelite tribes would be settling in the mountain regions of Judah, Samaria, and Galilee; and the Philistines would occupy the Mediterranean coast of southern Canaan. Classic battles would be fought between Israelites and Philistines during the days of Saul and David. The slave people who were just escaping from Egypt were not yet ready for battle with the Philistines, so "God led the people round by the way of the wilderness toward the Red Sea" (Exod. 13:18). With the pillar of cloud by day and the pillar of fire by night, God brought the people from slavery to freedom.

As the Israelites were leaving Egypt, Pharaoh again changed his mind. With the chariots of Pharaoh behind them and the waters of the Red Sea (literally, "Sea of Reeds") before them, Israel was again in desperate straits: "Then Moses stretched out his hand over the sea; and the Lord drove the sea back by a strong east wind all night, and made the sea dry land, and the waters were divided" (Exod. 14:21). The hosts of Pharaoh were overwhelmed. Moses had brought his people out of Egypt. One series of problems was past, another yet ahead. Israel must still survive in the wilderness.

Moses is known as the leader of the Exodus and as Israel's lawgiver. Having crossed the Red Sea, and commemorating that crossing in a song of triumph (Exod. 15:1-18), Moses and the Israelites entered the Sinai Peninsula. Again we are in the realm of the miraculous. God provided food for the Israelites in the form of manna from heaven, and water was miraculously provided from the rock which Moses was told to strike (Exod. 17:6). The people also ate the quail which came and covered the camp (Exod. 16:13).

The first challenge to Israel came from the Amelekites (Exod. 17:8). Victory came through prayer and work. Joshua, later to lead the Israelites into Canaan, was leader of the Israelite fighting men, while Moses, Aaron, and Hur went to the top of the hill at Rephidim. As long as Moses' hands were lifted in prayer the Israelites prevailed. As Moses grew weary they put him on a stone and Aaron and Hur held up his hands, one on each side. Thus the Israelites prevailed against the Amalekites.

In the vicinity of Horeb, Moses was reunited with Jethro, his father-in-law, who was convinced that Moses was working too hard. Jethro urged him to appoint judges to care for the more routine matters so that Moses could give attention to important matters (Exod. 18:18-26). Moses accepted the advice and appointed able men to share his responsibilities.

Three important events took place while Israel was encamped at Mount Sinai (1) the law was given; (2) Aaron and his sons were anointed to serve as priests; and (3) The tent of meeting, or tabernacle, was erected as the meeting place between God and His people.

The genius of Moses is accountable on the basis of his divinely provided preparation and divine inspiration. He was a man of tremendous ability who had had the finest education available in Egypt. Moses used that education in doing the work God gave him to do. Education was not enough, however. Moses went to Mount Sinai where he had a direct encounter with the Lord. Moses was the mediator through whom the law was given to Israel, but it was God's law (Exod. 20:1). The God of history, who had brought His people from slavery to freedom, demanded the absolute loyalty of His people. They must revere His name and honor His sabbath day. In their relations with one another, His people must respect their parents, honor the gift of life itself, and consider marriage sacred. A man has a right to own his property, and circulating lies about one's fellow man is deemed sinful. Even the attitude of coveting a neighbor's wife or possessions is itself a violation of the law (Exod. 20:1-20).

The law is a declaration of principles. Specific penalties for violations of the law come with the ordinances that follow (Exod. 21 ff.).

It was under the leadership of Moses that the distinctive elements of Israelite faith were developed. The tent of meeting was built, its sacrificial system and officiating priesthood regularized, and concepts of worship that date back to man's earliest years were formalized (cf. Gen. 4:3-4). The tent of meeting was a portable shrine suitable for use during the wilderness wanderings, but its basic functions were to be incorporated into the temple built in the days of King Solomon. Law would always be related to the person of Moses.

Moses had led the Israelites from Egypt to Sinai where the law was given, the tent of meeting built, and Aaron solemnly consecrated as high priest. Here, too, Israel entered into solemn covenant with their God. He had shown Himself to be their God, and they would be His people.

After the encampment at Sinai, the Israelites under Moses moved northeastward toward the land of promise. From Kadesh-barnea, near the border between Sinai and Canaan, Moses sent spies representing the twelve tribes (Num. 13). The spies searched the land and returned with a divided report. All agreed that Canaan was a good land. They brought back the grapes of Eshcol as evidence of the abundant fruit. The majority of the spies, however, reported that the inhabitants of the land were strong and gigantic. The Israelites were like grasshoppers in comparison with these giants. Caleb was ready to trust God and move toward Canaan. The majority ruled, however, and so the Israelites turned back into the wilderness. The pilgrims became wanderers; the travelers became tramps. The generation that left Egypt perished in the wilderness.

We have only a few episodes recorded for the forty years of wandering. A man named Korah and his followers rebelled against Moses' leadership, but they were killed when "the ground under them split asunder" (Num. 16:31). Again and again the people murmured against Moses because they were dissatisfied with the food and the scarcity of water. On one such occasion the Lord told Moses to tell the rock to yield its water for them and their flocks. In anger, however, Moses struck the rock twice with his rod (Num. 20:2-13) and water gushed out.

The Lord was displeased with Moses because of this, and said, "Because you did not believe in me, to sanctify me in the eyes of the people of Israel, therefore you shall not bring this assembly into the land which I have given them." Moses would not live to bring the people into the promised land.

At the end of the forty years, Moses and his people determined to enter Canaan from the east journeying northward through Transjordan. They went around the land of Edom when the Edomites refused them passage, but they fought and defeated the Amorite king Sihon who had his capital at Heshbon (Num. 21:21-35). This was a major battle, and the Israelite victory terrified the Moabites and the Midianites who looked for ways to stop the oncoming army of liberated slaves.

Balak of Moab sought to employ a man named Balaam from northern Mesopotamia to curse Israel, but Balaam could utter only blessings (Num. 22-24). The Moabites did bring a curse on Israel by inviting the Israelites to take part in the licentious Baal fertility cult. This ritual prostitution was counter to all that Moses had stood for, and he ordered the participants slain (Num. 25:1-5). Sad to say, Baal worship was to become a continuing snare to Israel.

Moses' death came in the plains of Moab,

opposite Jericho. From Mount Nebo he viewed the promised land, but he did not live to enter it. At the age of 120, still in possession of all his faculties, Moses died and was buried somewhere in the land of Moab opposite Beth Peor (Deut. 34). By every definition, Moses was a giant of faith. He could be angry and impatient on occasion, but it was his leadership that united a band of former slaves into a people in solemn covenant with their God.

QUESTIONS

1. What peoples in modern times find in Moses inspiration for their freedom?

2. Why did Pharaoh not wish to give the Israelites their freedom?

3. What influence, if any, did Jethro have on Moses?

4. How was Moses prepared for his mission as Israel's lawgiver?

5. Moses did not live to enter the promised land. Are you conscious of modern parallels? Name them.

5 JOSHUA
Conqueror of Canaan

Joshua ben Nun—Joshua the son of Nun—was the heir to Moses in leadership of the Israelite tribes. Moses had brought them out of Egypt, through the wilderness, and to the borders of the promised land. It was Joshua who had the responsibility of bringing them into Canaan and organizing the tribal confederation.

PREPARATIONS

Moses had been the instrument through whom God gave His law to Israel. Joshua, too, would hear God's commission. He must "go over this Jordan" (Josh. 1:2) and bring the Israelites into the land which had been promised centuries before to Abraham and his descendants. God demanded courage as well as faith. Joshua must cross the Jordan and enter the land. "Every place that the sole of your foot will tread upon I have given you" (Josh. 1:3) was the divine promise. This was not a passive waiting for God to act. It was active faith—stepping into the water and moving into the promised land with the assurance that God would honor His promises. Joshua and the people of Israel must be faithful to God's law. God would honor their faith with victory (Josh. 1:8).

As a practical matter, Joshua sent two spies from his camp in Moab, east of the Jordan, to the strongly fortified city of Jericho, west of the Jordan. Jericho was an oasis in what came to be called the Judean Wilderness. The city has been fortified since prepottery neolithic times, as Kathleen Kenyon's excavations have shown. Since the dawn of history any invader from Transjordan would head for the "city of Palm Trees" where there were adequate supplies of water. If Israel was to enter Canaan from the east, Jericho must be taken.

The spies made their way to the house of Rahab, the harlot of Jericho. Harlots have been used in military espionage throughout history. Rehab, however, saw in the mission of the spies the hope of a new life. She had heard about the miraculous opening of the Red Sea before the Israelites, and of their victories over Sihon and Og in Transjordan (Josh. 1:9-14). Rahab "by faith" (Heb. 11:31) hid the spies from their enemies. In return, they agreed that she and her household would be spared when the Israelites took Jericho.

The actual crossing of the Jordan was, like the crossing of the Red Sea, a miracle. The priests, bearing the sacred ark of the covenant, entered the river, whereupon the waters were held back at a place named Adam, permitting the Israelites to cross over on dry land (Josh. 3:14-17).

Entering Canaan was a decisive moment in Israel's history. Joshua commanded that stones be taken from the Jordan River, and these were built into a memorial monument set up at the encampment site of Gilgal on the west side of the Jordan. The monument would remind future generations of God's faithfulness in bringing His people safely across the Jordan (Josh. 4:19-24).

The encampment at Gilgal marked a new beginning for Joshua and Israel. The rite of circumcision, neglected during the wilderness wandering, was reintroduced (Josh. 5:2-7). The manna which had miraculously fed the Israelite encampment in the wilderness ceased. Now that Israel was in the promised land they could eat the fruit of the land of Canaan (Josh. 5:10-12).

THE CENTRAL CAMPAIGN

The land belonged to Israel by promise, but many battles were ahead before it would belong to Israel in fact. The first battle was for Jericho, the key to central Canaan. Once again Scripture speaks of a miracle. God gave Jericho into the hands of Joshua by way of a very strange type of siege. Each day the Israelite army marched around the city. Seven priests bearing their trumpets (the *shofar*, or ram's horn) went before the ark of the covenant at the head of the procession. On the seventh day they blew the trumpets after marching around the city seven times. At that point the walls of Jericho fell flat and Joshua took the city (Josh. 6:1-21).

Rahab and her family were spared, but otherwise the entire city was destroyed (Josh. 6:22-25). Jericho was the first city of Canaan to fall to the Israelites, and its destruction was total. Joshua and his armies next followed the valley northwestward from Jericho in the direction of Bethel. There a battle which should have been a minor one was fought at a place "near Beth-aven, east of Bethel" (Josh. 7:2) known as Ai. To the consternation of Joshua and the Israelites, the men of Ai were victorious. Again, Israel is not judged for poor military tactics, but for disloyalty to the Lord. An Israelite had stolen some of the spoil of Jericho. As long as the sin was unpunished, Israel would flee before her enemies (Josh. 7:1, 10-15). A man named Achan was identified by lots as the guilty one. He and his family were stoned in the valley which came to be called "The Valley of Achor" (trouble) (Josh. 7:22-26).

After the death of Achan a second battle for Ai was fought, and this time the Israelites were successful. The city was left a heap of rubble (Josh. 8:28). The success of the central campaign was such that Joshua assembled the tribes in the region of Shechem between Mount Ebal and Mount Gerizim. With the priests divided, half before Mount Gerizim and half before Mount Ebal, Joshua read the blessings for obedience and the curses for disobedience, along with the entire Mosaic law (Josh. 8:30-35).

Israelite victories at Jericho and Ai had a psychological influence on other Canaanite cities. The people of Gibeon decided to accept the Israelite presence in Canaan without fighting. To trick Joshua into making an alliance, they pretended they had come from a great distance. With ragged clothes, moldy bread, and broken wineskins they succeeded in making Joshua agree to an alliance. When the deception became known, Joshua still accepted the terms of the alliance. The Gibeonites would live in the midst of Israel, but they would become "hewers of wood and drawers of water" for the Israelites, and for the sanctuary in particular (Josh. 10:16-27).

Joshua obligated himself to protect the Gibeonites, and he was called upon to do so very quickly. An alliance of kings from the south determined to punish the Gibeonites for making peace with Joshua. They understandably reasoned that one after another of the Canaanite towns would accept Israelite rule, with the result that the land would be lost to the Canaanites.

THE SOUTHERN CAMPAIGN

The king of Jerusalem, Adonizedek, with his allies, the kings of Hebron, Jarmuth, Lachish, and Eglon, marched northward against Gibeon. The Gibeonites sent word of their danger to Joshua who was at the Israelite encampment at Gilgal. Joshua responded at once, marching his armies all night and surprising the coalition of kings from the south at Gibeon. The attack from the south was turned into a rout as Joshua chased the survivors through the Valley of Beth-horon toward Azekah and Makkedah (Josh. 10:5-11). To compound the problems of the

Canaanites, a hailstorm occurred which was of such intensity that more were killed in the storm than by the armies of Israel. Joshua rejoiced in this further evidence that God had intervened on behalf of His people. With so momentous a victory, Joshua prayed for more time to finish the destruction of the Canaanites. He prayed, "Sun, stand thou still upon Gibeon, and thou, Moon, in the valley of Aijalon" (Josh. 10:12).

This event is quoted in the Book of Joshua from an ancient, evidently poetic book of Israelite history known as the Book of Jashar (Josh. 10:13), which recorded the events of this unique day. Israel gained a decisive victory and with it effective control of southern Canaan.

The final campaign was in the north where Jabin of Hazor led the final desperate attempt of the Canaanite leaders to stop the Israelites. Again, Joshua's victory was total (Josh. 11:1-15). For all practical purposes the conquest was over, although important pockets of resistance would remain until the time of David. During the time of the judges, Israel would have to defend herself against a succession of foes. The Philistines were the most troublesome, continuing as Israel's foes throughout Old Testament times.

Following the conquest, Joshua and the elders of Israel assembled for the division of Canaan among the tribes. Each received an allotment which can be identified on the map of the division of the land among the tribes. The Levites were the priestly tribe. They did not have a regular allotment, but had cities assigned to them among the tribes.

Joshua's last act was at Shechem where he assembled the tribes for a covenant renewal ceremony. The former generation had received God's law at Sinai. Now the generation that had conquered Canaan must ratify that covenant for themselves. Joshua urged them to make a choice. His own choice was clear: "As for me and my house, we will serve the Lord" (Josh. 24:15b). The people followed his example, although Joshua warned them of the dangers of disobedience (Josh. 24:19-20). At the age of 110 Joshua died. He had successfully carried on as Moses' successor. Israel was now in Canaan.

QUESTIONS

1. Spies were sent by both Moses and Joshua in preparation for the conquest of Canaan. Can espionage be morally justified? Does it show a lack of faith?

2. How did life in Canaan differ from life in the wilderness for the Israelites?

3. Was Joshua right in honoring his treaty with the Gibeonites even though they had deceived him?

4. Achan stole some of the spoil of Jericho with the result that the Israelites suffered defeat at Ai. Why was this considered such a serious offense?

5. Why did the Canaanites fight with Joshua? Are there modern parallels?

6 SAMUEL
King Maker

Samuel appears as a bridge between the period of the judges when "every man did what was right in his own eyes" (Judg. 21:25) and the monarchy with its centralized and, at times, absolute government. We first meet his mother Hannah in her moments of anguish. She regards herself as a failure because she is childless. In agony of soul she prays, "O Lord of hosts, if thou wilt indeed look on the affliction of thy maidservant, and remember me, and not forget thy maidservant, but wilt give to thy maidservant a son, then I will give him to the Lord all the days of his life, and no razor shall touch his head" (I Sam. 1:11).

Hannah's prayer was made in the house of God at Shiloh. There the portable shrine which had been moved from place to place during the wilderness wandering was set up on a more permanent basis. A priest named Eli with his two sons, Hophni and Phinehas, officiated at the house of God.

As Eli saw Hannah move her lips in prayer without uttering audible words he accused her of being drunk. The very accusation says something of the spiritual state of the land. Hannah properly rebuked Eli, explaining the nature of her prayer. Eli then gave her his blessing and Hannah, confident that the Lord would grant her request, returned home joyfully. "And Elkanah knew Hannah his wife, and the Lord remembered her; and in due time Hannah conceived and bore a son, and she called his name Samuel, for she said, 'I have asked him of the Lord' " (I Sam. 1:19-20).

After Samuel was weaned, Elkanah and Hannah brought young Samuel to Eli at Shiloh. She had vowed that the child would be dedicated to God, and now she was prepared to leave him at the house of the Lord. She saw him once a year when she came for the annual sacrifice. She would bring along clothing which she had made for her son during the time of their separation ((I Sam. 2:19). After the birth of Samuel, Hannah was blessed with three other sons and two daughters (I Sam. 2:21).

While Samuel's environment in the house of the Lord should have been of the best, this was not the case. Eli's sons were wicked. In their greed they would take for themselves the best part of offerings brought by the people (I Sam. 2:13-17). They introduced the Canaanite fertility cult worship into the worship of the Lord (I Sam. 2:22). Ritual prostitution, which was an important part of the worship of the Canaanite Baal, was abhorrent to loyal worshipers of the God of Israel. Eli's sons are called "sons of Belial," or worthless men (I Sam. 2:12).

One night young Samuel heard someone calling his name. He naturally thought it was Eli and hastened to the aged priest to find out what he wanted. No, Eli had not called. It happened a second time, and a third. The third time Eli sensed that God was calling Samuel, and he told the lad to reply, "Speak, Lord, for thy servant hears" (I Sam. 3:9). God responded with a message concerning Eli and his household. Eli's priesthood would come to an untimely end, for his sons would not follow in priestly office. When Eli learned what God had said to Samuel he offered no objections: "It is the Lord; let him do what seems good to him" (I Sam. 3:18).

The end of the family of Eli is associated with the battle of Aphek. The Israelites were suffering at the hand of the Philistines and in desperation they sent to Shiloh to bring the ark of the covenant from the house of the Lord to the battlefield. They looked on it as a good luck charm. Certainly God would not allow this sacred ark to fall into the hands of the enemy! But they were wrong. The Philistines fought harder than ever, captured the ark, and routed the Israelite army. Among the casualties were Hophni and Phinehas.

When a messenger brought news of the disaster to Eli, the aged priest "fell over backward from his seat by the side of the gate; and his neck was broken, and he died, for he was an old man, and heavy" (I Sam. 4:18). Today we would say that he had a heart attack. The wife of Phinehas died in childbirth, but her son survived. His name, Ichabod ("no glory"), was a comment on the tragedy of defeat: "The glory has departed from Israel, for the ark of God has been captured" (I Sam. 4:21).

To the dismay of the Philistines, the ark did not bring them good luck. They put it in the temple of their god Dagon, but the statue of Dagon fell face downward before the ark. Dagon's head and arms were severed from the trunk of the statue (I Sam. 5:1-5). When the people were afflicted with tumors, the men of Ashdod decided to send it to another Philistine city, Gath. When things turned for the worse in Gath, they sent it to Ekron. Finally the people of Ekron sent it with a guilt offering to Beth-shemesh, a border city between Israel and the Philistines. From Beth-shemesh the ark was brought into Israelite territory by the men of Kiriath-jearim, modern Abu Ghosh, west of Jerusalem. There it remained until the days of David, who brought it to his new capital at Jerusalem.

With the death of Eli and his sons a power vacuum was evident in Israel, and consequently Samuel's gifts and piety became obvious. He urged the people to reject the Baals and the Ashtaroth (I Sam. 7:3), fertility cult idols, and to serve the Lord only. At Mizpah the people gathered with Samuel to confess their sins and to renew their covenant of loyalty to the Lord. As Samuel was offering the burnt offering, the Philistines attacked (I Sam. 7:10). This time, however, the forces of Israel prevailed. Samuel had been God's spokesman in bringing about a spiritual revival. The Philistines were caught off guard and thrown into confusion, not knowing what hit them (I Sam. 7:10). Israel regained territory that had been lost to the Philistines (I Sam. 7:14). A monument was erected to commemorate the victory. It bore the name Ebenezer, "stone of help," for Samuel said, "Hitherto the Lord has helped us" (I Sam. 7:12).

As Samuel was growing older he had the love and loyalty of his people. They were concerned, however, about his sons who "turned aside after gain; they took bribes and perverted justice" (I Sam. 8:3). The Philistine threat was still real and the elders of Israel wanted to be sure of adequate leadership after Samuel's death. They asked Samuel to appoint a king to govern them as other nations were governed. The theocracy—the rule of God through judges—seemed inadequate (I Sam. 8:4-6).

Samuel was heartbroken. This seemed a rejection of all he stood for; but God said, "Hearken to the voice of the people in all that they say to you; for they have not rejected you but they have rejected me from being king over them" (I Sam. 8:7). Samuel warned the people of the ways of kings (I Sam. 8:10-18). Monarchy frequently means despotism—absolute power corrupts absolutely! Nothing is sacred to kings—property, children, even "you shall be his slaves." When ruled by a despot you might "cry out because of your king, whom you have chosen for yourselves; but the Lord will not answer you in that day." This is an important principle with modern application. The totalitarian state is easy to get into, hard to be delivered from. When we make choices we must be aware of the consequences.

The people would not be dissuaded, so preparations were made for the anointing of Israel's first king, Saul, the son of Kish of the tribe of Benjamin. Both Saul and his successor David are honored as great kings, yet both were guilty of the kind of crimes Samuel had warned about.

Samuel must have been thoroughly disillusioned as the time of his death approached. Saul had been rejected by God because of his disobedience. The Philistines were again a threat to Israel, profiting from the rivalry between Saul and David. Samuel is a Biblical hero in his own right: "all Israel . . . mourned for him, and buried him in Ramah, his own city" (I Sam. 28:3). Much of his story is part of the stories of Saul and David.

QUESTIONS

1. Why was Hannah concerned about the fact that she had no child?

2. Why was Eli weak as a priest and a parent? To what extent are parents responsible for the sins of their children?

3. Why did the Philistines want the ark? Why did they want to get rid of it?

4. Why did the Israelites want a king?

7 SAUL
King Who Began Well

Saul, son of Kish, was a handsome young man of the tribe of Benjamin when the elders of Israel asked Samuel to anoint a king. In physical appearance Saul towered over other people—the kind of man the Israelites could literally look up to. He seemed to have the qualities that would mark a good king. He was also humble in those days—always an admirable quality.

The Bible introduces us to Saul in three episodes. In the first we read that the asses of Kish were lost and he sent his son Saul with a servant to find them. After a diligent search they were about to give up. Saul's servant, however, learned of a man who had the reputation of being a prophet. Perhaps he could help them find the animals.

In the meantime God had prepared Samuel for his visitors. The day before Saul's arrival the

Lord had said to Samuel, "Tomorrow about this time I will send to you a man from the land of Benjamin, and you shall anoint him to be prince over my people, Israel" (I Sam. 9:16). When they met, Samuel told Saul not to worry about the lost animals. He had more important business. A sacrificial meal was prepared in preparation for the solemn anointing of Saul as Israel's first king (I Sam. 9:15—10:1). As token of Saul's new position he gave evidence of the gift of prophecy (I Sam. 10:9-13). Until then, however, only Samuel and Saul knew that Saul had been designated king.

Next we read that Samuel gathered the people at Mizpah. The tribes were brought forward to determine by lot the Lord's choice as Israel's king. The lot fell on Saul, but he was nowhere to be found. He had hidden himself among the baggage, but when he was found Samuel publicly proclaimed him as king (I Sam. 10:20-24).

In the third episode, Saul publicly leads the Israelite tribes to victory over a cruel oppressor (I Sam. 11:1-11). The Ammonite king Nahash had besieged Jabesh-gilead, threatening to gouge out the eyes of its inhabitants (I Sam. 11:1-5). Saul rallied the tribes, attacked the Ammonites, and saved Jabesh-gilead. The beginning of his reign seemed to indicate the wisdom of the people in requesting a king.

Problems between Samuel and Saul soon developed, however. The Philistine threat was again real, and the Israelites prepared for battle. Saul waited seven days for Samuel to come and offer the burnt offering and the peace offering before battle. When Samuel did not appear, Saul presumptuously offered the sacrifice himself. This was regarded as a violation of the distinction between the prerogatives of king and priest or, as we would say, between church and state. Israel had been given a king, but he must be subject to the Torah, the law of God. A king had no right to intrude into priestly functions.

When Samuel appeared he charged, "You have done foolishly, you have not kept the commandment of the Lord your God, which he commanded you" (I Sam. 13:13). Saul's sin was so great that the kingship would not continue in his family. God would choose another to succeed him.

A second break between Saul and Samuel took place following a decisive battle with the Amalekites. Saul had been commanded to destroy the Amalekites and all their property; but he spared Agag their king and the best of their sheep, oxen, and other possessions (I Sam. 15:1-10). He rationalized this act to Samuel with the assertion that the people saved the best of the sheep and of the oxen "to sacrifice to the Lord your God" (I Sam. 15:15). From Samuel's viewpoint this was disobedience: "Has the Lord as great delight in burnt offerings and sacrifices as in obeying the voice of the Lord? Behold, to obey is better than sacrifice, and to hearken than the fat of rams. For rebellion is as the sin of divination, and stubbornness is as iniquity and idolatry. Because you have rejected the word of the Lord, he has also rejected you from being king" (I Sam. 15:22-23).

Samuel then ordered that Agag, the Amalekite king, be brought to him. He revealed

God's sentence on him in these words: "As your sword has made women childless, so shall your mother be childless among women" (I Sam. 15:33). What Saul had refused to do, Samuel did: "And Samuel hewed Agag in pieces before the Lord in Gilgal" (I Sam. 15:33b).

For all practical purposes the usefulness of Saul as a king was over, although he would continue to reign many years. Saul acknowledged his sin of disobedience to Samuel (I Sam. 15:24), but Samuel was convinced that there was no hope for Saul. The Lord had taken the kingdom from him and would give it to another (I Sam. 15:28).

From here on the story of Saul and that of David overlap. Samuel went to Bethlehem where he anointed Jesse's youngest son, David, to become Israel's new king. Knowing nothing of this, Saul in his fits of depression had discovered that musical therapy proved helpful. David was asked to become a member of Saul's household, "and whenever the evil spirit from God was upon Saul, David took the lyre and played it with his hand; so Saul was refreshed and was well, and the evil spirit departed from him" (I Sam. 16:23).

The once powerful Saul was now mentally ill. Some have suggested that we would term his sickness a manic-depressive psychosis. In Biblical thought, all that comes into our lives—bad as well as good—comes through God's will. If Saul was insane, in Biblical language this was evidence that God had afflicted him.

Young David soon became a popular hero. He had killed the Philistine champion Goliath of

Gath (I Sam. 17:31-54), as well as proving consistently successful in his attacks on all of Israel's enemies (I Sam. 18:1-5). The women sang of David's exploits: "Saul has slain his thousands, and David his ten thousands" (I Sam. 18:7). David was ten times better than Saul! David might appreciate such acclaim, but how about Saul? Jealousy got the better of him, and he determined to kill David. In a fit of insanity Saul threw his spear at David, but David successfully escaped.

There is irony in the relations between Saul's family and David. Jonathan, Saul's son, might well hope to succeed his father as king. But we see no hint of jealousy in Jonathan's dealings with David. On the contrary, the two became the best of friends. Jonathan gave his robe, his armor, his sword, his bow, and his girdle to David (I Sam. 18:3) in token of his admiration and friendship. Jonathan's attitude puzzled his father. With David a potential rival for the throne, how could Jonathan befriend him? Yet Jonathan risked his life for David, and the friendship of these two has become one of our finest examples of human loyalty.

The love of Saul's daughter Michal for David is readily understood. The young princess falls in love with the magnificent warrior. Saul heard about it and was pleased—for the wrong reasons! David would be expected to pay a bride price for the hand of Michal. Saul would appear to be very generous and patriotic. Kill a hundred Philistines, and as evidence bring me their foreskins, and Michal will be yours (I Sam. 18:25-26). Saul hoped, of course, that the

Philistines would kill David. David was more than successful: he returned with two hundred foreskins of the uncircumcised Philistines.

Saul now had but one goal in life—to kill David. Several times he nearly succeeded, but it was clearly God's will to save David to become Israel's next king. On one occasion Michal let David down through the window to escape from Saul's messengers (I Sam. 19:12). At another time Saul actually threw his spear at his son Jonathan in anger at Jonathan's loyalty to David (I Sam. 20:30-34).

David was now a refugee and Saul was in constant pursuit. Obviously, only the Philistines could prosper from this situation of a divided Israel. David fled into the Judean wilderness, but Saul followed him. On one occasion David had the opportunity to kill Saul. David and his men were in the innermost part of a cave, when suddenly Saul entered the outer part of the same cave! David crept toward the place where Saul was relieving himself, and cut off the skirt of Saul's robe (I Sam. 24:1-7). David would not allow his men to attack Saul. Indeed, his conscience even bothered him that he had cut Saul's skirt. While Saul would have been happy to attack and kill David, David kept the most profound respect for Saul as "the Lord's anointed."

After Saul left the cave, David identified himself to Saul, showing that he had had an opportunity to kill him. Saul seemed to be touched at David's generosity. He stated that he knew David was destined for the throne, and asked that David show compassion on his descendants. This David promised to do (I Sam. 24:16-22).

On another occasion David and a loyal follower, Abishai, stole into Saul's camp at night and found him fast asleep. David took Saul's spear and the water jar at his head, but again refused to do bodily harm to the Lord's anointed (I Sam. 26:6-25). Again David identified himself to Saul from a safe distance, and Saul appeared to be moved that David had shown compassion. Yet David knew that Saul's burning desire was to kill him.

David soon realized that he was safer with the Philistines than with his own people. He became a vassal of Achish, king of Gath; but he was careful never to attack his own people (I Sam. 27:1-12). In the meantime Saul's problems were growing. The prophet Samuel had died, so Saul could get no counsel from him. The Lord gave no word to Saul through dreams or urim or prophets (I Sam. 28:3-6). Saul felt so totally God-forsaken that he resorted to a practice which had been forbidden in Israel. He learned of a spiritistic medium at Endor; so he furtively made his way to her house, putting on a disguise to avoid detection. The medium was frightened, reminding the stranger that Saul had outlawed the work of the mediums. Saul vowed that no harm should befall her, and asked that she bring up Samuel from the abode of the dead.

What the woman then saw frightened her, but Saul told her not to fear. She described Samuel as "an old man . . . wrapped in a robe" (I Sam. 28:14). Samuel asked why Saul had disturbed him, and the king revealed that he could get no message from God. Samuel's reply was pointed: "Why then do you ask me, since the Lord has turned from you and become your enemy?" (I Sam. 27:16).

Samuel did not bear good news. The Philistines would be victors over the Israelites, and Saul and his sons would die on the battlefield. In the words of Samuel, "Tomorrow, you and your sons will be with me" (I Sam. 28:19). The kingdom would be taken from Saul and his family and turned over to David (I Sam. 28:15-19).

Saul's life came to an end in the battle with the Philistines on Mount Gilboa. We have two accounts of his death. In the first (I Sam. 31), when Saul was wounded he asked his armor-bearer to kill him with his sword. When the armor-bearer refused, Saul fell on his own sword and died. In the second (II Sam. 1), when Saul was wounded he asked an Amalekite standing nearby to kill him. The Amalekite obliged, taking Saul's crown and armlet, symbols of royalty, and gave them to David. Perhaps the Amalekite made up the story of his having killed Saul in expectation of reward from David. If so, he was badly mistaken. David ordered that he be killed for having killed "the Lord's anointed."

Saul, his three sons, and his armor-bearer all died at Mount Gilboa. The Philistines placed the captured armor in the temple of the goddess Ashtaroth, and fastened Saul's body to the wall of Beth-shan. The desecrated body would serve as a warning to others who might be tempted to challenge the Philistines! We read of a final act of heroism by the people of Jabesh-gilead. Saul's first act as Israel's king had been to relieve the people of Jabesh-gilead when they were besieged and threatened by the Ammonites (I Sam. 11).

They never forgot their debt to him; and now, as a final tribute to Saul, they stole out at night, removed the bodies of Saul and his sons from the wall of Beth-shan, brought them to Jabesh, and burned them. Cremation was not the normal means of disposing of the dead, but under the circumstances they could not risk further desecration at the hands of the Philistines. The remains were then buried under a tamarisk tree, and the people fasted for seven days.

Saul was a man of tremendous ability. He began well, and many in addition to the men of Jabesh-gilead must have been indebted to him. The positive side of Saul is evidenced by the fact that his name continues to be used as a name of honor. Another Benjamite of a later day, Saul of Tarsus, bore his name. We remember Saul's heroic earlier days, but we cannot forget the tragedies of his later years. Perhaps it is understandable that he was jealous of David, but when jealousy became an obsession that consumed his time, his energies, and in many ways his very life itself, we have a man whom God could not honor. Saul is a warning to all who start well. Disobedience, pride, jealousy cost Saul dearly. Oh, what a king he might have been!

QUESTIONS

1. What accounted for Saul's early popularity?

2. Did Samuel ever accept the idea that Israel should have a king? Was he anxious for Saul to make a mistake so he could remind them, "I told you so"?

3. What evidence do we have that Saul was mentally ill?

4. What influence did the Philistines have on politics within Israel?

5. Why were the Amalekites considered to be so wicked?

8 DAVID
Man After God's Own Heart

Young David is a very attractive person. We first meet him in the family of Jesse of Bethlehem. Samuel has come to anoint a king to replace Saul, whose disobedience to God has rendered him unacceptable (I Sam. 16:6-13). Jesse began with his oldest son, assuming that he would be the chosen one. The Lord, however, had other plans. Seven of Jesse's sons were brought to Samuel, but in each instance we read that the Lord had not chosen that one. When Samuel asked if he had seen all of Jesse's sons, Jesse replied, "There remains yet the youngest, but behold, he is keeping the sheep" (I Sam. 16:11). Samuel asked that he be brought in, and, sure enough, he was the one to be anointed as Israel's next king. The point is clear. The sovereign God chooses whom He will. Man might choose on the basis of the outward appearance, but God looks on the heart (I Sam. 16:7).

Our second encounter with David is in the court of Saul, where he was brought to help soothe one of the king's fits of insanity. Here we learn another side of David's character, that of poet and musician. History knows him as the psalmist, with almost half of the Biblical Psalms ascribed to him. His dirge over the death of Saul and Jonathan is one of the most moving poems of all literature. Young David as a skilled musician brought comfort and refreshment to the troubled king.

Our third view of the young David is on the battlefield meeting the challenge of Goliath of Gath. The Philistine champion had terrorized the Israelite army. No one would accept the challenge to meet him in single combat until David unexpectedly appeared on the scene with provisions for his brothers and the leaders of the Israelite forces. Having no armor or sword, David was thoroughly unprepared for battle. Yet he was horrified that there was no one among the hosts of Israel who would meet the challenge of this giant who had defied the armies of the living God. If none among the warriors would meet his challenge, then David would!

Saul's armor was offered, but David felt uncomfortable with it. Instead he took his staff and chose five stones from the brook to use with his sling. David would meet Goliath with nothing but a sling and five smooth stones. Goliath was insulted. What he didn't know was that David had taken too many stones. The first one reached its mark, hitting Goliath in the forehead. He fell on his face to the ground. Then David ran to Goliath, took the Philistine's sword from its sheath, and cut off Goliath's head with his own sword (I Sam. 17:17-54).

Things were going well with David. He became a popular hero and his praises were sung throughout the land (I Sam. 18:7). Popularity brings problems, and David soon learned that he had a major one. Saul was insanely jealous, and the king determined that David must be killed.

Saul's hatred for David did not prevent Jonathan, Saul's oldest son, from befriending him, nor his daughter Michal from falling in love with him. Saul could never understand his children, but he did try to use them to bring about the death of David. Nevertheless, threats and challenges did not divert David from his mission. David fought his people's enemies and gained victories on the battlefield until he had to flee into the Judean wilderness to escape the men of Saul who were seeking his life. On at least two occasions David could have killed Saul, but he would not lift his hand against the Lord's anointed.

David and his followers were forced to live off the land. We see an example in his dealings Nabal, a wealthy man with three thousand sheep and a thousand goats. David ordered his men not to interfere with Nabal's men, but David did expect a gift of provisions for his people. Nabal, however, was incensed at the suggestion that he give something to David: "Who is David? Who is the son of Jesse? There are many servants nowadays who are breaking away from their masters. . ." (I Sam. 25:10). As far as Nabal was concerned, David was simply an outlaw unworthy of respect or help. Nabal's wife Abigail saw things differently, however. She hastily prepared provisions for David and apologized for the conduct of her husband. David was impressed with Abigail and abandoned his plan to avenge the insult of Nabal.

When Abigail told Nabal what she had done, he was enraged. We read that "his heart died within him, and he became as a stone" (I Sam. 25:37). Nabal evidently suffered a stroke, and ten days later he was dead. David, whose wife Michal, Saul's daughter, had been given to another, wooed Abigail and she became his wife. Ahinoam of Jezreel was a second wife of David at about this period in his life (I Sam. 25:39-43).

The death of Saul and Jonathan in the battle of Mount Gilboa brought important changes for David. His best friend, Jonathan, and his most bitter enemy, Saul, were dead and the way was clear for David to claim kingship for himself. David ordered the death of the Amalekite who claimed to have killed Saul. Although the death of Saul and Jonathan removed obstacles to David's kingship, David genuinely grieved over their deaths, "Saul and Jonathan, beloved and lovely! In life and in death they were not divided. . ." (II Sam. 1:19-27).

Although his grief was genuine, the deaths of Saul and Jonathan were politically good for David. Had Jonathan not died, the possibility of rivalry between the two would have been real. As it was, a surviving son of Saul, Esh-baal (or Ish-bosheth as he is otherwise called), had the support of Saul's former military commander, Abner, and held on to the support of the northern tribes. The men of Judah acclaimed David their king at Hebron in the south (II Sam. 2:1-4). Among David's loyal followers was Joab, his military leader. During the fighting between the forces of Esh-baal and David, Abner killed Asahel, Joab's brother, and thereby began a blood feud (II Sam. 2:18-23).

The power of David increased at the expense of Esh-baal. Abner took to himself Rizpah, a former concubine of Saul, and Eshbaal interpreted this as a challenge to the throne. In anger, Abner left Esh-baal and transferred his loyalty to David. Even under normal circumstances a rivalry may have developed between Joab and Abner, but their relationship was not normal. Since Abner had killed Joab's brother, Joab felt justified in killing Abner (II Sam. 3:30). David mourned for Abner, but Joab was not challenged because he had acted according to the acknowledged principles of blood revenge.

Esh-baal's cause had grown progressively weaker until one day at noontime two men slipped into his bedchamber, killed him, and beheaded him. They thought David would honor them for killing his rival, but they were mistaken. At David's command the murderers were themselves killed, and Esh-baal was given proper burial beside Abner in Hebron.

Early in David's career everything seemed to favor him. He had nothing to do with the death of Saul and Jonathan, or of Abner, or of Eshbaal. He spoke well of them all and, except for Joab, ordered the death of those who had perpetrated the crimes. Those who had been loyal to the house of Saul could respect David for his behavior and without compunction give their loyalty to him (II Sam. 5:1-5).

For David to be able to rule efficiently over all twelve tribes, a more centralized capital was desirable. The Jebusite city of Jerusalem was ideally located. It had not been occupied by the Israelites, and for that reason was not within the boundaries of any tribe. Benjamin was to the north of Jerusalem, Judah to the south. David conquered the Jebusite stronghold, and Jerusalem has been sacred to the people of Israel ever since.

The Philistines became concerned when they learned that David had been anointed king over the twelve tribes. They moved into the Valley of Rephaim, southeast of Jerusalem, prepared to battle David. Two battles were fought, but David was victorious both times, chasing the Philistines completely out of the hill country (II Sam. 5:17-25).

With Jerusalem established as the political capital of the twelve tribes, David determined to make it the religious center as well. The ark was brought from Kiriath-jearim to Jerusalem with a joyous procession dancing before the Lord (II Sam. 6:1-23). This was perhaps the happiest moment of David's life. He was now the acknowledged king over all Israel, ruling from his new capital where the ark of the covenant was about to be placed in the tent which he had prepared.

One thing more would complete David's happiness. He had a splendid palace; should not God dwell in a splendid temple? David told his plans to his court prophet Nathan, and Nathan was at first enthusiastic. God spoke to Nathan, however. The prophet must tell David that God didn't want David to build Him a house (a temple). God, however, would build David a house (a dynasty). A son of David would succeed to the throne, and he would build the temple. When kings of the Davidic line would sin, they would be punished; but kingship would not be taken from the line of David as it had been taken from the family of Saul (II Sam. 7:4-17).

It is because of this promise to David that the New Testament mentions David as the ancestor of Jesus the Messiah. Any king over the people of Israel must be able to trace his lineage to David. True, the north seceded after the death of Solomon, but their kings were never regarded as legitimate rulers by the prophetic spokesmen of the south. During and after the exile in Babylon, the godly remnant looked for and prayed for a righteous king of David's line, an anointed one, or messiah. Christians affirm that Jesus of Nazareth is that Messiah. Greek-speaking Christians would say, Jesus is the Christ. He is the son of David in whom all the hopes of the faithful in Israel are centered. He is also the hope of the world.

David's kingdom extended far beyond the tribal boundaries as a result of victories over the Philistines, Moabites, Arameans, Edomites, and Ammonites. His territories reached the upper Euphrates, and all of the lands of Transjordan were subject to him (II Sam. 8). Tribute from these subject lands made Israel wealthy. By worldly standards, David had all he could desire.

Yet at this very moment, David's sin wrought havoc on himself and his whole people. His armies were besieging Rabbah, modern Amman in Jordan. Joab was out with the troops, but David was at home in Jerusalem. A good king was expected to be with his fighting men, but David was beginning to relax in his duties.

Late one afternoon, David looked from his roof and saw a beautiful woman bathing. He asked about her and learned that her name was Bathsheba, and that she was the wife of one of his soldiers, Uriah the Hittite. David sent for her, had sexual relations with her, and fathered a child. David acted without conscience in his relations with her, but now he tried to hide his crime.

David sent word to Joab to send Uriah home for a period of rest. When Uriah arrived in Jerusalem, David told him to go home—hoping of course that Uriah would have sexual relations with Bathsheba so that the child which she was bearing would be considered Uriah's child. Uriah, however, did not go home. He considered it inappropriate for him to enjoy the comforts and joys of his home while his companions were risking their lives in battle. He may also have shared the common view that sexual relations weaken a man and make him unfit for battle.

When David's plan for covering the results of his sin was thwarted, he took more drastic action. He sent orders to Joab to place Uriah in the thick of the fighting where he would be sure to be killed. Uriah carried the letter, and the ever loyal Joab did as he was told. Soon a messenger reached David with the news that a battle had been fought, and that the Israelites had suffered many casualties, and that among them was Uriah the Hittite.

David's response was thoroughly hypocritical: "Thus shall you say to Joab, 'Do not let this matter trouble you, for the sword devours now one and now another; strengthen your attack upon the city, and overthrow it.' And encourage him" (II Sam. 11:25). Casualties are a part of war. Too bad there were so many. Try harder next time, and I'm sure you'll gain the victory. Thus David dismissed the whole episode (II Sam. 11).

At this point God's prophet Nathan had something to say. There were two men, one rich, the other poor. The rich man had abundant flocks and herds; the poor man had but one ewe lamb. A guest came to the house of the rich man; but instead of taking of his abundance, he took the poor man's lamb to provide a meal for his guest. David as king should be able to make a judgment in such a case. The verdict came quickly: the man deserves to die. He must restore the lamb fourfold because he did this thing, and because he had no pity (II Sam. 12:1-6). It is so easy to judge others!

Nathan's reply was equally terse: "You are the man" (II Sam. 12:7). God made you king. He gave you all you could desire, and would have given you more if you had asked. You have despised the word of the Lord. You have murdered Uriah after having had adulterous relations with his wife. God's judgment will rest on you for the sins of which you are guilty.

Note that David is considered a murderer just

as truly as if he had killed Uriah with his own sword. It was his order that sent Uriah to his death. David acknowledged his sin, and Nathan assured him that his sin was forgiven, but its results would continue to plague David. His child by Bathsheba would die. Disoriented family life would plague him the rest of his days.

Bathsheba's first child died. After the death of Uriah David had married her and an affectionate relationship seems to have developed. He comforted her in the death of her child. Subsequently another child, Solomon, was born to David and Bathsheba; and he would one day become king (II Sam. 12:15-24).

Troubles did indeed develop within David's family. A son, Amnon, raped his half-sister Tamar. Absalom, Tamar's brother, then planned the death of Amnon, after which he fled to Geshur where he remained three years (II Sam. 13). Joab effected a reconciliation between David and Absalom, and the latter returned from exile, but he was never on good terms with his father.

Soon we find Absalom in open revolt against his father. He is now young and charming. As people come to him with their problems, he promises whatever they wish. His comment is common to political opportunists of all ages: "Oh that I were judge in the land! Then every man with a suit or cause might come to me and I would give him justice" (II Sam. 15:4).

Soon the nation was going through the throes of civil war. Absalom and his followers gained a large following—so large that David had to flee from Jerusalem. The king was torn between the desire to keep his throne and the wish that no harm befall his son Absalom.

Absalom's revolt came to an end as a result of a freak accident. He was riding his mule through the forest when his head was caught in the branches of the tree while the mule trotted on. A witness brought word to Joab, who was a matter-of-fact man of action. He took three darts and thrust them into Absalom's heart.

When word reached David that Absalom was dead, he was heartbroken. His victorious troops entered Jerusalem in silence as they learned that David was grieving for Absalom. Joab was clearly upset with David for his conduct. David was acting as though he wished Absalom were alive and all his faithful soldiers dead. David had better show his appreciation to his loyal troops or he would not be able to depend on them in another hour of need. Happily David saw the point. He sat at the gate and the people came to see their king (II Sam. 19:1-8).

David soon faced another revolt—this time from a man named Sheba, a Benjamite. Benjamin had been Saul's tribe; and there were those who looked on David, who was from the tribe of Judah, as an intruder. Again Joab pursued the rebel and besieged Abel of Beth-maacah, the city into which he had fled. Joab and his forces were prepared to batter down the walls and destroy the city when a wise woman intervened. She told Joab that the head of the rebel, Sheba, would be thrown over the wall. When this was done the siege was lifted and the revolt was at an end (II Sam. 20).

Israel's trials continued through the end of

David's life. There was a three-year famine (II Sam. 21) and a pestilence which came to an end after three days (II Sam. 24). David purchased the threshing floor of Araunah the Jebusite as a place for burnt offerings (II Sam. 24:21). Interestingly, this is the site on which Solomon later built the temple.

In his old age David became senile. His servants feared that he was sexually impotent so they brought a beautiful maiden as his nurse and companion. The king "knew her not" (I Kings 1:4), proving his impotence as a man and as a ruler. The question of succession was immediately faced; and Adonijah, David's son by his wife Haggith, with the support of Joab and other influential members of the court prepared to be acclaimed as David's successor. Nathan, however, supported Solomon. He told Bathsheba what Adonijah was planning. Bathsheba went to David, who assured her that her son Solomon was his choice for the throne. Adonijah's plan was thwarted as Solomon was anointed king (I Kings 1).

David's death came after a forty-year reign: seven years in Hebron and thirty-three in Jerusalem. We find in him some of the best and some of the worst qualities of mankind. He could be generous and loyal. His dirge over the death of Saul and Jonathan, and his mourning for Absalom show him to be a man of deep feeling. On the other hand his lust for Bathsheba and his judicial murder of Uriah show that he could be thoroughly oblivious to the law of God and ordinary decency expected in our dealings with fellow humans. That God can forgive even the murderer and adulterer is gospel truth. That our sins cause God's enemies to blaspheme and leave marks on our own lives as well as on the lives of others is illustrated in the career of David.

QUESTIONS

1. David, like Solomon after him, had many wives. Is he criticized for this? Why, or why not?

2. What evidence do we have of David's generosity toward his enemies?

3. Describe the relationship between David and Jonathan. Are there any hints of homosexuality?

4. In what sense was Joab a practical military man? How did he regard sentiment?

5. Account for the relationship between Joab and Abner. Was blood revenge a reason or an excuse for Joab killing Abner?

9 SOLOMON
Wise Man Who Ended Foolishly

Had Absalom not rebelled against David, he might have lived to become Israel's third king. As it was, when David showed signs of senility there were two contenders for the throne: Adonijah the son of Haggith and Solomon the son of Bathsheba. Adonijah had an impressive following, including Abiathar the priest and Joab, David's efficient military commander.

Nathan the prophet—who spoke so pointedly to David at the time of his sin with Bathsheba—now supported the claims of Solomon, and warned Bathsheba of danger to herself and her son if Adonijah became king. Unsuccessful contenders for the throne did not have a long life expectancy (I Kings 1:11-14). Bathsheba was to remind David that he had designated Solomon as his successor, and that he must act now to declare his choice publicly and thus thwart Adonijah's purpose.

David ordered that Solomon be anointed king. Nathan the prophet and Zadok the priest, joined by others loyal to Solomon, met at Gihon, east of Jerusalem in the Kidron Valley. Zadok the priest anointed Solomon, followed by the blare of trumpets and the shout, "Long live King Solomon" (I Kings 1:38-40).

When the partisans of Adonijah heard the sound of Solomon's partisans, they knew that their cause was hopeless. The coup they had planned was thwarted by David's direct action, and they were not prepared to challenge David. The best they could hope to do was to save their lives.

Adonijah went for refuge to the tent of meeting and took hold of the horns of the altar. He asked that Solomon swear that he would do no harm to him. Solomon was unwilling to grant unconditional amnesty. If Adonijah behaves himself, he will be safe. If he doesn't he will die. That was the most Adonijah could get from Solomon (I Kings 1:49-53).

After warning Solomon about his enemies, David died. Adonijah then went to Bathsheba, asking her to intercede with Solomon to grant Abishag the Shunamite—the girl brought to David in his old age—as a wife for himself. Bathsheba did not see the significance of the request, but Solomon did. Marrying the wife of the former king could be considered a claim to the throne itself. Solomon interpreted this as a treasonous plan, and promptly ordered Adonijah's death (I Kings 2:19-25). Abiathar, the priest who had been loyal to Adonijah, was expelled from his priestly position. Solomon also ordered Joab killed, ostensibly because he had killed Abner and Amasa, commanders of the armies of Israel and Judah. Benaiah became the new military commander, and Zadok the new high priest.

We may contrast the opening days of the reigns of David and Solomon. All of David's real or potential rivals were removed, but David did not harm one of them. Solomon's actions were direct. If they were a threat to him and his government, they must go. The author of I Kings notes that "the kingdom was established in the hand of Solomon" (I Kings 2).

Early in Solomon's reign, the king went to sacrifice at Gibeon, and the Lord appeared to him. God asked him to indicate the gift that he wanted, and Solomon asked for the gift of wisdom. He realized that he needed wisdom to rule God's people. The request implied humility on Solomon's part, and the Lord was pleased. Solomon would get the desired wisdom, and he would also receive honor and wealth (I Kings 3:3-14).

The wisdom Solomon requested was of a practical nature—wisdom to rule, wisdom to judge. Soon he had an opportunity to show his wisdom. Two harlots came to him. Each had borne a child, and one of the children had died. Each claimed that hers was the living child, and that the dead child belonged to the other. Solomon asked that a sword be brought to him so that he could divide the living child in two. The real mother then asked that the life of the child be spared and the whole child be given to the other claimant. In his wisdom Solomon declared that she was indeed the mother, and that the child should be given to her (I Kings 3:15-28).

Solomon gained the reputation of being the wisest of men. He uttered and collected proverbs, many of which are preserved in the Biblical Book of Proverbs (I Kings 4:29-34). The Queen of Sheba, in southern Arabia, came to the court of Solomon to see his splendor and hear his words of wisdom. She concluded that she had not heard half of the good things that could be said about Solomon and his court (I Kings 10:1-10).

Solomon gave attention to Israel's relations with her neighbors, and one method of making alliances was by marriage. Solomon married the daughter of the Egyptian Pharaoh—itself an evidence of the wealth and power of Solomonic Israel. Relations with Egypt were obviously cordial, and the Pharaoh must have considered Solomon at least an equal. The Pharaoh gave Solomon the city of Gezer, which continued as an Egyptian outpost in Israel until this time.

Hiram, king of the Phoenician city of Tyre, enjoyed commercial dealings with Solomon. The famous cedar wood from the Lebanon mountains was sold to Solomon for his building projects. We also read that Solomon imported horses, chariots, and exotic goods from Egypt, Cilicia, and perhaps even east Africa and India through trade routes from Ezion-geber into the Red Sea (I Kings 5:7-12; 10:23-29).

Solomon's great building project was the temple in Jerusalem. It was built during the golden age of Israel's material prosperity. The plan was basically that of the older portable shrine, the tent of meeting, or tabernacle. Now, however, a permanent building was erected on Mount Moriah, north of the Davidic city of Jerusalem. The best of materials were imported from all over the Near East to make the temple a structure worthy of Solomon's Jerusalem and the God of Israel. This very fact caused problems, for some would equate external splendor with spirituality, with the result that the doctrine developed that God would never allow his house to be desecrated (an idea that Jeremiah refuted). The wisdom of Solomon and his achievement in building the temple are the two positive things that are remembered about him.

Solomon's domestic policies were more controversial. He divided the land into twelve administrative districts (I Kings 4:7-19). He used forced labor on his building projects (I Kings 5:13; 9:15-22), and taxation, especially during the latter part of his rule, became unbearably high. His palace, the temple, chariot cities for the defense of the land, the splendor of his court—all these were gladly accepted by the people as long as tribute was coming in from distant parts of Solomon's empire. When the empire began to fall apart, however, and tribute was not coming in, resentment of Solomon's policies began to increase.

The latter days of Solomon, as of Saul and David, brought aggravated problems. Marriage alliances had increased in number. Solomon had married "the daughter of Pharaoh, and Moabite, Ammonite, Edomite, Sidonian, and Hittite women" (I Kings 11:1). He could boast seven hundred wives and three hundred concubines. Marriage alliances and the concept of splendor evidenced by an enormous harem account for the thousand wives and concubines. They came from many lands and worshiped many gods. Solomon himself became involved in their idolatry, and soon Jerusalem was dotted with shrines for "Ashtoreth the goddess of the Sidonians . . . Milcom the abomination of the Ammonites . . . Chemosh the abomination of Moab . . . Molech the abomination of the Ammonites" (I Kings 11:5-8) and others. The wise Solomon had allowed matters of political expediency to compromise his loyalty to the God of Israel.

Even before Solomon's death we see his empire beginning to disintegrate. Hadad, an Edomite prince who had fled to Egypt when David and Joab conquered Edom, returned home to lead Edom to independence from Solomon (I Kings 11:14-22). An Aramean prince, Rezon, challenged Solomon in the north (I Kings 11:23-25), and Jeroboam, an Ephraimite, challenged Solomon within Israel itself (I Kings 11:26-40).

Jeroboam was encouraged by a prophet, Ahijah of Shilo, who tore a new garment into twelve pieces and gave ten of them to him with the words, "Take for yourself ten pieces; for thus says the Lord, the God of Israel, 'Behold, I am about to tear the kingdom from the hand of Solomon, and will give you ten tribes' " (I Kings 11:31). Many of the prophetic leaders of Israel must have been thoroughly scandalized by the excesses of Solomon. It was only three generations since Saul reigned in rustic simplicity. Now

Jerusalem was a city of wealth, splendor—and idolatry.

Solomon tried to kill Jeroboam, but Jeroboam made his way to Egypt where he was granted asylum (I Kings 11:40). You will recall that early in Solomon's reign he was on such good terms with Egypt that a Pharaoh sent his daughter to Jerusalem to marry him. Now, at the end of Solomon's career, relations had so degenerated that an avowed enemy of Solomon could find sanctuary in Egypt.

Solomon's son Rehoboam thought he could continue Solomon's policies after his death, but he miscalculated the resentment of the people. At that same time Jeroboam returned from Egypt to challenge Rehoboam. When Rehoboam refused to give his word that the burdens of heavy taxation and slave labor would be lightened, Jeroboam led the northern tribes in open rebellion. The north declared its independence of the south and the Davidic dynasty. The kingdom was divided because of the policies of Solomon, even though Solomon did not live to see the division.

QUESTIONS

1. How did Solomon handle threats to his rule?

2. What, precisely, is the wisdom for which Solomon is famous?

3. Why did Solomon marry so many women?

4. What help did Solomon have in building the temple?

5. How did Solomon alienate large sections of the country?

10 ISAIAH
Evangelical Prophet

The first verse of Isaiah's prophecy tells us that he was active during the reigns of Uzziah, Jotham, Ahaz, and Hezekiah, kings of Judah. Uzziah's reign had been long and prosperous. Those who were well off had nothing to complain about. They could bring their sacrifices to the temple and meet the ceremonial demands of their religion. The plight of the fatherless and the widow did not concern them. The poor were powerless; so why worry about them? Isaiah of Judah and his northern contemporary Amos give us a pretty sorry picture of religious life during the days of Uzziah and his successors.

Prophets do not always talk about the future; often they look back. God brought His people out of Egyptian slavery and cared for them in their wilderness wandering. Moreover, He brought them into the land of milk and honey. The prophet bids us remember. He also bids us to remember our vows. We accepted His law. We vowed obedience and loyalty. God has been faithful to His word. How about us?

Prophets also have a disconcerting habit of holding a looking glass to the present. "The whole head is sick. . . . Your country lies desolate. . . . What to me is the multitude of your sacrifices . . . wash yourselves . . . cease to do evil" (Isa. 1:5-16).

Part of a prophet's message is to talk about the future. That future may be near: "The Lord will bring upon you and upon your father's house such days as have not come since the day that Ephraim departed from Judah—the king of Assyria" (Isa. 7:17). Judgment, especially in the form of the exile to Assyria and Babylon, were on the near horizon, and the prophets warned that it was imminent. Yet they also spoke of the more remote future—the Messianic age, the end time when a righteous king of the Davidic line would rule, when men would "beat their swords into ploughshares, and their spears into pruning hooks" (Isa. 2:4). The Messiah, the Savior will one day come. Look for Him. He is your hope. That was the prophetic message, too. Judgment is ahead—but beyond that, deliverance. So spoke Isaiah in harmony with the other prophets.

Isaiah tells us that his call came during the year that King Uzziah died. The prophet was in the temple when he saw a vision of the Lord. The entire atmosphere spoke of the exalted Lord attended by angelic creatures called seraphim. As the seraphim spoke of God's holiness, the very foundations shook and the smoke of incense filled the temple.

The reaction of Isaiah was immediate: "Woe is me! For I am lost; for I am a man of unclean lips, and I dwell in the midst of a people of unclean lips; for my eyes have seen the King, the Lord of hosts." Isaiah saw himself a sinner in the presence of a holy God. His reaction was similar to Peter's: "Depart from me, for I am a sinful man, O Lord." Consciousness of sin as an offense to a holy God is a first step in conversion.

One of the seraphim took a live coal from the altar and touched Isaiah's lips with it. You have sinned, yes. Your lips are unclean, yes. But the altar is there. The sacrifice has been made—your guilt is taken away, your sin forgiven (Isa. 6:7). A holy God has provided for the salvation of the lost: "though your sins are like scarlet, they shall be as white as snow" (Isa. 1:18).

Following Isaiah's conversion comes his commission. God has messages to send; so He needs messengers. Thankful for God's mercy, Isaiah volunteers, "Here am I! Send me" (Isa. 6:8). The task will be a thankless one. The prophet will pour his heart out, but the people won't know what he is talking about. The more they hear, the harder their hearts will be; but there will be a small remnant that will respond. That will make the prophet's ministry worthwhile.

As a court prophet, Isaiah sought to give an encouraging word to Ahaz at the time of the Syro-Ephraimitish War. Syria and Ephraim (=Israel, the Northern Kingdom) formed an alliance against Ahaz of Judah because he would not join them in an alliance against Assyria. Their plan was to remove Ahaz and put their man, Ben Tabeel, on the throne of Judah. Isaiah with his son Shear-jashub (a label name meaning "A remnant shall return") went to meet Ahaz as he was checking the water supply of the city. In the event of a siege an adequate water supply is essential. Isaiah told him not to worry about the kings of Syria and Israel, for they were only smoking firebrands. Within a short time Damascus and Samaria would fall. God would not allow Ahaz to be defeated.

Ahaz was weak in faith, but Isaiah urged him to trust God with the assurance that the lands of his two enemies would soon be deserted. The king of Assyria would change the entire political situation (Isa. 7:1-18).

During the reign of Ahaz, Hoshea came to the throne in Samaria. He was to be Israel's last king. Samaria fell to Assyria during Hoshea's ninth year, and Israelites were carried into exile (II Kings 17:1-6). This must have been quite a shock to the people of Judah. The tribes to the north had been forcibly taken away, and Assyria was occupying territory to the north. Would Judah fall?

Samaria fell in 722 B.C. and in 701 B.C. the armies of the Assyrian king Sennacherib were in Judah. Most of the land had fallen but Jerusalem held out. This time Isaiah encouraged King Hezekiah with the assurance that God would protect Jerusalem. Hezekiah was a man of greater faith than Ahaz. He stood his ground against Sennacherib, and the Assyrians had to lift their siege. Second Kings states that "the angel of the Lord went forth and slew a hundred and eighty-five thousand in the camp of the Assyrians; and when men arose early in the morning, behold these were all dead bodies" (20:35). Sennacherib returned home where sometime later he was murdered by two of his sons.

Hezekiah gained the reputation of being a strong anti-Assyrian leader. Babylon, to the south of Assyria, had been subject to Assyria; but in times of Assyrian weakness, Babylon was able to go her independent way. During Hezekiah's sickness, Merodach-baladan of Babylon sent envoys with letters and a present to Hezekiah, who felt highly honored. He showed the envoys his treasures and armor; but Isaiah warned him that the time would come when Babylon, not Assyria, would be a threat to Jerusalem (II Kings 20).

With the death of Hezekiah, we lose track of Isaiah. Hezekiah's successors, Manasseh and Amon, were idolatrous rulers; and so Isaiah's message would not have been welcome at that time. Tradition suggests that Isaiah died a martyr's death.

No prophetic book is quoted more frequently than Isaiah. Matthew quotes Isaiah 7:14 in presenting Jesus as the virgin-born child named Immanuel ("God with us"). Isaiah 9:6 speaks of the child to be born who would sit on the throne of his father David and whose name would be Wonderful, Counsellor, The mighty God, The everlasting Father, The Prince of Peace. Isaiah 53 describes the suffering servant of the Lord who was "wounded for our transgressions . . . bruised for our iniquities" (v. 5). Isaiah brings words of comfort (40:1) as well as warning (24:1-4). We know little about his personal life except that he was married and had at least two children (7:3; 8:1-4). It is his message that has left its deepest mark on subsequent generations.

QUESTIONS

1. Is there a necessary connection between prosperity and neglect of God? Why do people turn to God in times of adversity rather than in times of prosperity?

2. Prophets are usually thought to be foretellers of the future. Why is such a definition inadequate?

3. Isaiah received his call in the temple. Can you think of other Biblical characters whose call came at other places?

4. There were numerous crises during Isaiah's time. What comparable crises do we face today?

5. Did Isaiah reject the concept of animal sacrifice? What disturbed him about organized religious life in his day?

6. Compare Ahaz and Hezekiah as rulers. With whom did Isaiah enjoy the better relations?

7. In what sense can the word *evangelical* be applied to Isaiah?

11 JEREMIAH
Prophet No One Would Believe

We know more about Jeremiah's personal life than about any of the other prophets. He was from a priestly family of Anathoth, northeast of Jerusalem and, like Isaiah, was a court prophet. He began his prophetic ministry in the days of Josiah, the last of Judah's godly kings. He prophesied until the destruction of Jerusalem, and spent his last days in Egypt.

Jeremiah's call is described briefly in the first chapter of his book: "Before I formed you in the womb I knew you, and before you were born I consecrated you; I appointed you a prophet to the nations" (Jer. 1:5). The concept of God's eternal purpose is particularly relevant in times when the very foundations of society seem to be crumbling. Such was the situation in Jeremiah's day, and he often needed to remind himself of God's purpose for his life.

The first reaction of Jeremiah was negative: "Ah, Lord God! Behold, I do not know how to speak, for I am only a youth." His humility was commendable, but he was forgetting that God would put His words in his youthful mouth. Jeremiah would be God's spokesman and he would bring both words of warning and encouragement to God's people. But Jeremiah would speak more words of warning than of encouragement (see Jer. 1:10).

Jeremiah went to the temple in Jerusalem, stood at its gates and uttered his words of warning. Judah must turn from its evil ways if it is to survive. It is vain to trust the words of false prophets who say, "This is the temple of the Lord, the temple of the Lord, the temple of the Lord" (Jer. 7:4). The error was the inference that was being drawn from these words. In essence the people were saying that God would never allow Jerusalem to fall, but would protect His temple under all circumstances. Other cities of Judah might fall, as they did in the days of Hezekiah; but God would never allow Jerusalem to be destroyed. It was a comforting thought, but Jeremiah knew it was wrong.

It is easy to see why Jeremiah was so unpopular. Kings, priests, false prophets, common people—all regarded him as disloyal for daring to suggest that Jerusalem might fall. Knowing the judgments that soon would befall Judah and Jerusalem, Jeremiah did not marry (see Jer. 16:1-4). He was a lonely man who knew fellowship with his God, but even God seemed to forsake him (see Jer. 12).

Jeremiah tells of an encounter with Pashur,

the priest who was chief officer in the temple. Pashur beat Jeremiah and put him in stocks. When he was released the next day, Jeremiah repeated his prophecy, saying that all Judah would be carried to Babylon, and that Pashur and his family would die there in the land of their exile (Jer. 20:1-6).

Another encounter was with Hananiah, a prophet from Gibeon who was uttering optimistic predictions. This was during the reign of Zedekiah, when many exiles were already in Babylon. Hananiah said that within two years all the exiles, including King Jehoiachin, would be back in Judah. The yoke of the king of Babylon would be broken.

Jeremiah stated that he wished this prophecy were true, but he knew it was not. Time would soon prove whether Hananiah or Jeremiah had the true word from God. Jeremiah acted out his prophecy by wearing yoke-bars on his neck. Hananiah removed the bars and broke them, symbolizing God's breaking the yoke of Nebuchadnezzar. The Lord gave a message to Jeremiah. Hananiah ought to know that he could easily break a wooden yoke, but God would put an iron yoke of servitude to Nebuchadnezzar on the neck of the nations. The death of Hananiah ended this prophetic dispute (Jer. 28), but it is significant in showing the various voices which were seeking the ears of the people of Jerusalem. Both Jeremiah and Hananiah professed to be prophets of the Lord. Time proved that Jeremiah was right.

The prophecies that Jeremiah was uttering were conditional in nature. He spoke of doom, but held out hope if the people would turn from their evil ways: "Thus says the Lord: 'If you will not listen to me, to walk in my law which I have set before you, and to heed the words of my servants the prophets whom I send to you urgently, though you have not heeded, then I will make this house like Shiloh, and I will make this city a curse for all the nations of the earth' " (Jer. 26:4-6). The people demanded that Jeremiah be put to death for such words; but happily, reason prevailed. Some of the elders remembered that Micah had prophesied in the days of Hezekiah that Zion would be plowed as a field and Jerusalem would become a heap of ruins (Jer. 26:16-18). These were strong words but Hezekiah had not put Micah to death.

While the false prophets were saying that the exiles in Babylon would soon return, Jeremiah told them to prepare for a long stay. Not two, but seventy years would be the length of the exile. Jeremiah wrote a letter urging the exiles to become good citizens of the land of their exile. Marry, raise families, build houses, plant gardens, seek the welfare of your community, and pray to the Lord on its behalf. This is Jeremiah's counsel. Do not listen to the false prophets and diviners who are striving to stir you up into political rebellion. Accept the yoke of the king of Babylon (Jer. 29:1-9).

Yet Jeremiah's very word of pessimism has a note of optimism. You will not be in Babylon forever. Most of the exiles themselves would die in Babylon, but their children would return. God's promises of the restoration of the Davidic dynasty would be realized. A righteous branch would be raised up. He would reign as king, deal wisely, and execute justice and righteousness in the land (Jer. 23:5). God will one day make a new covenant with His people, writing His laws on their hearts. All will know the Lord. He will forgive their iniquity, and remember their sin no more (Jer. 31:31-34).

Jeremiah was so convinced that exiles would return that he purchased a field at Anathoth. He had the purchase documents properly sealed and had them deposited in an earthenware vessel—a kind of safe-deposit box—where they would one day be discovered and given to his heirs (Jer. 32:9-15).

Jeremiah lived to see his direst predictions come true. With the approach of Nebuchadnezzar's armies the Egyptians sent aid to Judah, and for a time it looked as though the Babylonians would be defeated. At that time Jeremiah was imprisoned because of his pro-Babylonian—or so they were interpreted—policies. The Egyptian armies abandoned the fight, however, and Nebuchadnezzar marched on Jerusalem. Jeremiah's word was consistent. It is futile to fight Nebuchadnezzar. God has given Jerusalem into his hand.

When the Babylonians took Jerusalem they destroyed the royal palace and the temple. Jeremiah was treated kindly because of his counsel of submission to Nebuchadnezzar (Jer. 39). A man named Gedaliah was appointed governor of those who remained in Judah, but a group of diehards murdered him and killed the Babylonian soldiers who were with him. Those of the Jews who were left decided that they should flee to Egypt. Jeremiah counseled them not to go, but they took Jeremiah with them as they fled to Egypt.

As far as we know, Jeremiah spent his last days in Egypt. He has been called "the weeping prophet," with good reason. He saw impending judgment, warned of it, but his message was not believed. Later generations would acclaim him as an inspired prophet, but his own generation chose to believe the words of the optimists who prophesied what the people wanted to hear.

QUESTIONS

1. Why was Jeremiah so unpopular?

2. Should he have been more diplomatic when he addressed the public?

3. Why did Jeremiah urge acceptance of Babylonian rule? Was he being disloyal to Judah in doing so?

4. What would be the grounds for putting Jeremiah to death?

5. Was it a sign of weakness in the God of Israel to allow Nebuchadnezzar to destroy the temple?

12 DANIEL
Displaced Person

The Babylonian exile was one of those episodes that leaves its mark on all subsequent history. To the conquered peoples, Nebuchadnezzar must have appeared as a despot, forcing an unwanted foreign rule on an unwilling people. Conversely, Nebuchadnezzar thought of himself as a thoroughly civilized, judicious ruler bringing enlightenment to people who would otherwise be ignorant barbarians.

The exile of Judah did not take place all at once. The Book of Daniel tells us that it was during the third year of Jehoiakim that Daniel and his companions were taken to Babylon (1:1). The very victory of Nebuchadnezzar must have been shattering to the faith of many. Could not the God of Israel give victory over this pagan worshiper of Marduk? Daniel knew that the Lord is all-powerful, but he also knew that for

His own purposes He sometimes does things we do not understand. For the moment it was enough to know that "the Lord gave Jehoiakim king of Judah into his hand, with some of the vessels of the house of God; and he brought them to the land of Shinar, to the house of his god, and placed the vessels in the treasury of his god" (Dan. 1:2).

Not only were treasures taken, but people were taken, too. Not all the people, but only select people—the very best. Later others would go, but this time Nebuchadnezzar wanted members of the royal family and the nobility. He wanted young people who were sound in body and alert in mind, "competent to serve in the king's palace." They would learn "the letters and language of the Chaldeans" (Dan. 1:4).

For the moment Nebuchadnezzar's program seemed humane enough. Captive youths would go to school in Babylon and prepare for government service. They would be well treated, and eventually they would forget they had been transported to a strange land against their will. This, at least, was Nebuchadnezzar's hope.

Daniel and his companions had to react to three phases of Nebuchadnezzar's program: school, new names, and a new diet. Where possible, they would cooperate. In matters of faith, they would draw the line.

Their training would take three years (Dan. 1:5). They would learn to read books in the dialect of Akkadian, which we call Neo-Babylonian, in the cuneiform script which goes back to Sumerian times. This would provide them with the key to a knowledge of Babylonian science and literature. They knew from their Bibles the Genesis account of creation. Now they would be taught the story of how Marduk cut in two the monster Tiamat and made heaven and earth from the two parts of her body. They would learn about astrology and medicine, about Babylonian law and mathematics. Some of this would challenge beliefs that they had held from childhood. What was their reaction to the training program?

We do not read of any objection. Centuries before, Moses had gone to school in Egypt where the God of Israel was looked on as an enemy. Moses had used that pagan education in the service of the Lord as the leader of the Exodus and as Israel's lawgiver. Daniel and his friends would do their best to excel in school.

Another aspect of Nebuchadnezzar's program was the assigning of Babylonian names to Daniel and his companions. Their Israelite names honored the God of Israel, but new names were assigned honoring the gods of Babylon. Daniel was given the name Belteshazzar. This was supposed to usher in a new era of his life. The old life in Judah must be forgotten. He would now be a good Babylonian. We do not read that the youths made any issue over the names. Among themselves they used their Hebrew names (see Dan. 2:17, 18), but they answered to their Babylonian names when so addressed.

The third aspect of acculturation into Babylonian ways was the matter of diet: "The king assigned them a daily portion of the rich food which the king ate, and of the wine which he drank" (Dan. 1:5). Here Daniel felt he had to draw the line. Babylonian food would not comply with Jewish dietary laws—it wasn't kosher. Daniel determined not to compromise his obedience to the Biblical laws, but he wanted to be as reasonable as possible in his request. He asked the prince of the eunuchs for permission to eat a vegetable diet instead of "the king's rich food." The prince of the eunuchs was favorably disposed toward Daniel, but he feared that he would be accounted responsible if Daniel's diet should make him weaker than those on the diet the king had prescribed. Daniel came up with a thoroughly reasonable solution. Let Daniel eat his own kosher diet for ten days. At the end of that time, Daniel could be compared with the others. Ten days is a very small fraction of three years. Any possible harm could readily be remedied. On the other hand, ten days should be long enough to determine whether Daniel could safely continue on his kosher diet.

Daniel's request was granted, and after ten days it was seen that Daniel and his companions were "better in appearance and fatter in flesh than all the youths who ate the king's rich food" (Dan. 1:15). God honored the faithfulness of Daniel and his friends. Their food was doubtless more wholesome than that which the king had prescribed, as the health of Daniel and his companions proved.

At the end of the three-year training program, Daniel and his friends were brought before the king. He was impressed with their wisdom and understanding, finding them "ten times better than all the magicians and enchanters that were in all his kingdom" (Dan. 1:20).

During the second year of his reign, Nebuchadnezzar made an apparently unreasonable request of his wise men. They must describe to him a dream he had dreamt and then forgotten, plus its interpretation. When the king threatened to kill the wise men because they could not tell him his dream, Daniel interceded on their behalf. No, he was not wise enough to do what the king demanded, "but there is a God in heaven who reveals mysteries" (Dan. 2:23) and Daniel was the medium through whom that God was speaking to the king. The king had seen a great image made of a variety of materials from the head of gold to the feet of iron and clay. The image represented a succession of empires following Nebuchadnezzar, represented by the head of gold. A stone would smite the image and break it in pieces. The stone represented the kingdom which God would set up on the ruins of the earthly kingdoms (Dan. 2). Nebuchadnezzar was so impressed with Daniel's ability that he honored Daniel and spoke of Daniel's God as God of gods, and Lord of kings.

In another dream, Nebuchadnezzar saw a tree which grew and became strong, providing shade for the beasts of the field and offering shelter for the birds in its branches. Then the tree was cut down, with nothing but its stump remaining. Daniel interpreted the dream as prophetic of Nebuchadnezzar's experience. The great king would be humbled. He would dwell with and act like the beasts of the field until he would acknowledge the Most High as ruler of men. Then he would be restored to his kingship. Daniel's interpretation was true, for the king spent a period of time afflicted by a mental disorder which made him think himself to be an animal. Recognizing the King of heaven as Sovereign of the universe, Nebuchadnezzar was restored to sanity (Dan. 4).

After the death of Nebuchadnezzar, Daniel continued to be highly regarded as a wise man in Babylon. When Belshazzar put on a licentious feast during which he desecrated the vessels from the Jerusalem temple, a mysterious handwriting appeared on the wall. Belshazzar was alarmed, and promised high honors to any who could read and interpret the writing. The queen suggested that Daniel, a man of great repute during the reign of Nebuchadnezzar, be brought in. Daniel disclaimed any interest in the king's proffered rewards. Instead, he spoke of the way God had humbled Nebuchadnezzar, and warned Belshazzar that he had not humbled himself before God. Then he read the words:

MENE   MENE   TEKEL   PARSIN

As nouns these can represent coins: a mina, a mina, a shekel, a half-shekel. As verbs they mean "numbered, numbered, weighed, divided." Daniel interpreted them as verbs: God has *numbered* your kingdom, and finished it; you are *weighed* in the balances and found wanting; your kingdom is *divided* and given to the Medes and Persians (Dan. 5). Belshazzar was slain that very night, and the Persian Empire took over Babylon.

Daniel's faithfulness continued into Persian times. Persian officials were jealous of him, but they could find no conduct of Daniel that would give them grounds for complaint. They finally decided that his religion might provide a way of getting at him. Approaching Darius, the king, they suggested that he make it a criminal offense for anyone in the kingdom to make petition to any god or man save Darius for a period of thirty days. The king's vanity was touched, and he signed the edict. Those guilty of violating the law would be cast into a den of lions.

Daniel did not hesitate to pray facing Jerusalem as had been his custom three times a day. His enemies felt that they now had caught him in violation of the law, although the king respected Daniel and hoped there would be some way to save him. Daniel was placed in the den of lions. When morning came he was found safe. His accusers were devoured by the lions, but Daniel himself had suffered no harm (Dan. 6).

Perhaps the characteristic most obvious in the stories of Daniel is his steadfastness. Daniel "continued" (Dan. 1:21) until the reign of Cyrus. He began well in his youth. He had to adapt to the policies of the Babylonians, and then to the new Persian regime. He had to face jealous local officials and wicked rulers, but he continued faithful to his God.

QUESTIONS

1. Did Daniel have respect for King Nebuchadnezzar?

2. Why was diet so important to Daniel?

3. What can we learn from Daniel's conduct toward the prince of the eunuchs? Are there contemporary applications?

4. Does the Christian in a secular school today face any problems comparable to those of Daniel in Babylon? Does Daniel provide any guidance?

5. Daniel obeyed the law of the land whenever he could do so in good conscience. Where did he draw the line? Is it ever right for Christians to refuse to obey the law? Cite examples from the New Testament. Suggest occasions when you feel disobedience might be proper today.

13 EZRA AND NEHEMIAH
Leaders of the Return

The Babylonian Empire came to an end with the Persian conquest of Babylon. Cyrus of Persia issued a decree permitting all Jews who desired to do so to return to their homeland (Ezra 1:1-4). Jeremiah's prophecies had proved true. The exile had lasted a long time; but a new government, with new policies toward captive peoples, was now in control.

Some of the Jews had done well in Babylon. All did not return to Judah at the first opportunity, and some had no desire at all to return. Some profited in business; others, like Nehemiah, attained high positions in government. Many parallels can be drawn between modern Zionism and this earlier ingathering of exiles.

Two names emerge as leaders among the Jews during this first period of resettling Judah. In many ways these men were very different, but their goals were identical. Ezra was a priest, and Nehemiah a layman. Ezra returned with a company of Jews from Babylon; Nehemiah kept his position in the Persian court and visited Jerusalem on a short-term leave of absence.

Under a man named Sheshbazzar the first company of Jews left Babylon for Jerusalem. Their expectations must have been great as they saw themselves fulfilling the prophecies of restoration from exile that Isaiah, Jeremiah, and other prophets had uttered. They found a ruined and desolate Jerusalem and a local population of adversaries who did everything possible to thwart their plans. Nevertheless they set up an altar and commenced to rebuild the temple (Ezra 3), but the "adversaries of Judah and Benjamin" used every tactic to delay the building. They accused the Jews before Artaxerxes, now king of Persia, of being a rebellious people and suggested that the Persians were making a mistake in allowing the Jews to resettle Jerusalem. The building temporarily ceased while the Persians investigated the charges. When the decree of Cyrus permitting the return was discovered, the work of building was resumed; but valuable time had been lost. The temple was completed in the sixth year of the Persian king Darius (Ezra 6).

During the reign of Artaxerxes a second company of Jews returned from Babylon. This group had as its leader a priest named Ezra, "a scribe, skilled in the law of Moses" (Ezra 7:6). He had authority delegated by Artaxerxes to make full provision for the reinstitution of the temple worship. He brought back vessels that had been taken to Babylon by Nebuchadnezzar, and also had funds to purchase anything necessary for the temple (Ezra 7:11-28).

Jerusalem now had a temple but problems continued. The city had no walls, and thus was open to attack from every side. Nehemiah, cupbearer to Artaxerxes in Susa, heard of the plight of his fellow Jews in Judah and asked the king for a leave of absence to help them (Neh. 1:1—2:10). Artaxerxes granted his request and ordered that aid be given Nehemiah in his long trip from Susa, in Persia, to Jerusalem.

When Nehemiah arrived in Jerusalem he inspected the ruined walls and gates to get some idea of the task ahead. Then he approached the people, explaining the reason for his visit and recounting the marvelous provisions God had made for his journey. The people were enthused at what God was doing in their midst, and they said, "Let us rise up and build" (Neh. 2:11-18).

Opposition was not long in appearing, however. Sanballat the Horonite, Tobiah the Ammonite, and Geshem the Arab tried everything from ridicule to guerrilla warfare to frustrate the Jews who were rebuilding the walls of Jerusalem. It was necessary for the builders to have their swords at their sides, but the work went on (Neh. 4:1-20). When they saw that they could not stop the building, Sanballat and Geshem tried to lure Nehemiah to a meeting with them, at which time he would doubtless have been murdered. He replied, "I am doing a great work and I cannot come down" (Neh. 6:1-4).

In spite of constant harassment, the walls were completed, and Jerusalem could now function as a city. Both Ezra and Nehemiah were devoted to the law of God, and they desired the restored Jerusalem to be wholly loyal to Scripture. They were convinced that disloyalty had brought on the exile. The restored people must live according to God's law.

Ezra brought a copy of the law to a public square before the water gate and read God's word to the assembled people from morning till night. He read from a wooden pulpit and, along with others who assisted him, "gave the sense so that the people understood the reading" (Neh. 8:1-8). The language of the law (Hebrew Torah, Greek Pentateuch) was Hebrew. The common language of the Jews who returned from exile was the language used in Babylon at that time—Aramaic. Ezra and his colleagues read the law in the Hebrew, then gave the sense in the Aramaic language of the people. These Targums, as they came to be called, mark the beginning of Bible translation. At first they were strictly oral explanations of the meaning of Scripture. We would call them paraphrases. Later they were written for the literate Jews to read.

Among the problems faced by both Ezra and Nehemiah among the Jews in Palestine was that of mixed marriage. Nehemiah was scandalized when he heard the children of Jerusalem speaking the language of Ashdod (Neh. 13:24). In any voluntary movement of peoples, the men usually precede the women. Evidently many of the men who had come to Jerusalem married women of Ashdod, Ammon, and Moab (Neh. 13:23). Nehemiah, with his devotion to the law of God, could not understand how such a compromising situation could develop. Even the wise King Solomon was led into apostasy by his foreign wives (Neh. 13:26). The only solution Nehemiah saw was to take a stand against all mixed marriages. We should remember, however, that the reasons for this were religious rather than ethnic. It was possible for a woman, like Ruth, to become a worshiper of Israel's God and become a part of the people of Israel. Idolatry, however, was an evil that could not be tolerated.

Nehemiah was horrified to find that a son of the high priest had married a daughter of Sanballat, one of the most bitter enemies of the Jews. In the words of Nehemiah, "I chased him from me" (Neh. 13:28).

Another problem that Nehemiah faced was sabbath observance. He observed men treading wine presses on the sabbath day. Trade and commerce was conducted on the sabbath as on other days (Neh. 13:15-18). Nehemiah ordered that the gates of Jerusalem be shut at sundown the day before the sabbath, and remain shut until after the sabbath was over (Neh. 13:19-22).

Ezra, Nehemiah, and the other spiritual leaders of their generation helped to make the Jews the people of the Book. They feared a repetition of the idolatrous practices that brought on the Babylonian exile, and they took drastic measures to ensure compliance with the Biblical law. This produced the possibility of another kind of sin—self-righteousness—and we know that such attitudes developed in all too many of the successors of Ezra and Nehemiah. This does not minimize the greatness of these men. They provided the leadership and the discipline needed by a people making a new beginning. Most of them had been born in Babylon. Now, in Judah, they must live pure lives in obedience to God's law. Although ruled by the Persian Empire for the time being, they looked forward to the day when a King of the Davidic line would reign in righteousness during the Messianic Age. The struggling Jewish community to which Ezra and Nehemiah ministered was a far cry from the kingdom of which the prophets spoke, but it was a beginning. The God who had fulfilled prophecy by bringing His people back to their land would fulfill prophecy yet again by sending to this people His anointed, His Messiah, the Savior of the world.

QUESTIONS

1. Why did many Jews choose not to return to Judah after the edict of Cyrus permitting them to do so?

2. What did those Jews who returned to Judah expect to find there?

3. How would you judge the treatment of the Jews by the Persian rulers?

4. Why would many of the inhabitants of the land resent the return of the Jews? Are there parallels in modern history?

5. Ezra and Nehemiah both faced the problem of mixed marriages. How should we approach this problem today?

6. Failure to observe the sabbath was another problem. Does this have any application to Christians today?